VICTORY LINER 504

Navy Daze: From Dark to Light, Revisited

JAAK TALLINN

EXPRESSO
Executive Center 777, Dunsmuir Street Vancouver, BC V71K4
1-888-721-0662 ext 101
info@expressopublishing.com

TABLE OF CONTENTS

Sailors in the Hanger Bay of the USS Flint (AE-32)

Dedicated to the 'Buds', and their many Filipino and Asian wives, as well as the sailors, marines, and 'seals' who served 'active duty' aboard US Navy ships in the South China Seas, South Pacific, and Indian Ocean (WESPAC) during the Vietnam war in the early to mid '70's. Also, to Matt, Boyd, and 'Crazy Joe', to whom I promised a copy of this book well over 40 years ago.

BOOT CAMP

"qualche santo provvederà"

Life is like a business. There is profit and loss, risk and reward. It requires investment in time, resources, and assets to realize benefits. You need cash flow. More in, … less out, to meet expenses and payroll. We invest in ourselves, and others as we grow. Yet, we constantly struggle to know ourselves better as we hope and pray that 'the saints will provide', and that everything will work out okay in our quest for our own independence.

So, perhaps that's what I was pondering during that critical car crash along highway 101 somewhere south of Crescent City, California on that temerarious early morning tear in early 1973 that prompted me to pen the poem 'Loose Ends'. What was my name? Was I really in the Navy? And, just who was this little guy sitting next to me on the grassy knoll near a pile of bent metal where we had somehow just disgorged ourselves from a twisted wreck? I learned that he had hit the pole doing 65 MPH after losing control in a hairpin turn, driving southbound down the coast. After the car spun out, the pole impacted the starboard side where I had been enjoying the morning sun, smashing my crown like a crushed avocado through the passenger-side window. He said that he knew me, and that he knew how to drive; but he didn't. He said that he had beaten on my chest for ten minutes because I had stopped breathing. He thought my neck was broken. He thought I was dead. "Unconscious for ten minutes", he said. "Really"? It was a magnificent morning, as I recall. I just wanted to get away.

My starboard ear was torn, I was picking glass out of my face and hair, my eye was cut, and I drew a blank as I tried to focus on the small crowd across the road that had gathered to gawk at the tangled wreckage.

They stood staring next to their Volkswagen mini-bus that was about to take us up the mountainside to a plastic surgeon's office where I would be examined further, and patched up. We had been heading south, but now we seemed to be heading north. I was confused. What was happening? They laid me on the examination table at the doctor's office in the surrounding hills where the plastic surgeon began to pick the glass out of my face, hair, and ears, and sew me up. It was so surreal. Who was I? "Relax. It's all going to be just fine". My head was still spinning when the police arrived at the doctor's small mountain office door and asked who was driving the rental car? The sailor that was with me told the cop that it was the other sailor who was still back at the hotel, who just happened to walk through the door, right behind the cop. It got a little complicated after that. We took a Greyhound bus back to San Francisco the following morning after the other two sailors filed a police report explaining how it all had happened. Someday, I would like to read that report.

I believe that my life changed forever on that fateful spring morning drive.

Or, perhaps my desire to put pen to paper was the result of the layoff several months earlier due to the slow economy, and my reluctance to take the 'Steamfitter's test' in Detroit. My Dad had made the necessary arrangements for me to take the test on three separate occasions, but each time I had decided to go drinking with my friends at our favorite neighborhood bar near Grand River and Lahser road instead. I was the only 'non-union' guy in the shop, the owner's son, and a disinterested worker in any case. My Dad needed to lay off someone, and union rules dictated that I should be the one to go. It would be a good lesson. I was OK with that. I had already decided that I didn't really want to be a 'steamfitter' for the rest of my life anyway. I had worked the previous year for the telephone company in 'station repair' and 'line sheets', repairing lines, installing phones, cutting in new terminals, splicing pick cable, running drop lines, replacing P-clamps, and climbing telephone poles around Farmington, Michigan after the construction crews came through, and decided that I wasn't cut out for a life with 'Ma Bell' either. I was taking flying lessons at a local airport during the same period that I was climbing telephone poles. I had also dropped out of the Air Traffic Control academy later that year, after a short trist with a cute little gal from Tennessee who thought that I might provide a regular source of income for a while. The people at the Air Traffic Control school were pissed. They needed new blood. I was a young licensed pilot with good grades in the class, so they weren't too happy when I resigned just two months after the courses started. Graduates of the school were slated to work in the various 'Control Centers' around the country upon graduation from the class. No way! Too stressful! The local college courses that I took at the time weren't working out very well either. Nor did the trek to California and back with one of my buddies later in 1969. After his '55 Ford panel truck broke down in Santa Rosa for the last time, we sold the truck for ten bucks to a young guy walking down the street, packed a pair of 'button up' levis, some underwear, a jacket, and a shirt into our sleeping bags along with a donated copy of 'The Hobbit', and hitchhiked south to LA. I rented a Cessna 150 for ten bucks at the county airport that we passed on our way out of town, just to get a 'birds eye' view of the California countryside before heading back down the road. They asked whether I had "a current medical". I said "yes"; then they tossed me the keys from behind the counter. We flew around the Santa Rosa area for about 45 minutes, and landed again at the airport. I was 20 years old. I turned 21 in LA, and could finally drink legally. From Los Angeles, we hitched back to Detroit through the desert and the plains, panhandling along the way, for the remainder of the summer of '69. I just didn't have any long-term interest in anything tangible in those early years.

After my Dad laid me off from his shop, I hopped into my yellow '59 corvette and drove down to the local recruiter on Grand River avenue one sunny day a couple of years later and announced "I want to be a doctor". They inquired about my experience. I told them that I knew how to fix refrigeration equipment. So, they signed me up as a 'Marine Mechanic' in their DPPO (Direct Procured Petty Officer) program for 'Machinist Mate' for 6 years in the 'Reserves'; 2-1/2 years active duty. Upon discharge, I could return to college on the GI Bill while on inactive duty. It sounded like a good plan, and a reasonable investment at the time. I would be in the CB's they said. I said "OK". My Dad said "don't leave that car sitting around the yard" while you're gone, ... so I sold the corvette for $800 bucks in the summer of 1972, prior to leaving for boot camp.

Then again, it's possible that I scribbled the first poem, with the analogous prose, based on events prior to leaving for boot camp with another buddy of mine, to share one last 'going away' beer. It didn't help that he was now part of the local law enforcement and wanted to experiment with his newfound power after five guys in a Cadillac 'flipped us the bird' as we turned the corner off McNichols road heading north on Outer Drive. I was quite surprised when my buddy pulled the nickel-plated pistol from his belt and pointed it across my nose at the five guys in the black Caddy, and shouted at them to pull over. Of course, they didn't know that Ricky was a cop, so after we made the U-turn heading south they forced his blue Camaro up over the grass median at a red light with their Cadillac, which resulted in a scuffle in the middle of the intersection with Ricky yelling that he was a 'police officer', when someone punched him in the face. I missed that part because I was going for the gun that was flying around the front seat of the Camaro at the time, as we fought for the pistol. I lost. Ricky stood there in the southbound lane in his six-foot frame with blood streaming down the front of his white T-shirt as they proceeded to march us both across the intersection with the gun pointed at my head, and into an abandoned gas station on the corner. Luckily, the guy that had taken the gun, wallet, and badge away from Ricky, had the good sense to remove the bullets after we had fought for it in the front seat of the Camaro. Otherwise, the little blond guy, who appeared to be hopped up on drugs at the time, and who eventually grabbed the gun away, would have blown Ricky's brains all over the gas station wall after he told him that he 'didn't care that he was a cop', and was going to kill him anyway, then pulled the trigger 3 times. Click, click, click. Nothing. That is, nothing other than the two squad cars from the local precinct that had just screeched into the gas station full of Detroit cops scrambling with their guns drawn, forced us up against the outside wall to sort things out. But that's a long story, which finished favorably in the end because Ricky was a cop. The last I saw of the little long- haired blond guy was after the cops beat the living hell out of him and pulled him down from the bonnet of their squad car where he had been jumping up and down on the hood, yelling to everyone how he hated '(expletive) pigs'. They handcuffed his legs and arms, threw him in the back seat, and headed toward the jailhouse. My buddy and I never did enjoy that last "going away" beer. I headed for boot camp a few weeks later instead.

Boot camp was a bust. I ended up in the Naval hospital twice, for almost a week each time, while going through basic training in Orlando, Florida. Once, because the idiots-in-charge had me standing watch over some white hats (i.e., the 'dixie cups' that sailors wear on their head, that can also be used as a flotation device), drying in the sun on a black rooftop in the 110°F Florida heat in September of 1972. I got 'sunstroke' with a 105°F fever, and they checked me into the base hospital. They ordered me to take a cold shower and drink a gallon of water every hour to bring my body temperature down. I spent 5 days in a hospital bed before being released back to my company. I had to fake my temperature to get out of the hospital because I couldn't stomach the thought of eating another piece of cold pizza. I was getting sick. More marching. More training. More, learning how to speak Navy. A mop is a swab. A floor is a deck. A staircase is a ladder. A wall is a bulkhead. A bed is a rack. A hat is a cover. Left is port, right is starboard. If it moves, salute it. If it doesn't, paint it. Like that.

I believe that the premise of the whole exercise was to get us all to work as a team, while building individual confidence in ourselves. After I recovered a bit, they had us join teams for 'sports week'. I was the pitcher on our company baseball team. It was good duty. I liked to pitch, although I was also good at first base. It all went well until one day, while fielding a pop fly in front of home plate, the fat little catcher blasted through me trying to beat me to the ball. I had called it. He was just stupid. In any case, the pain was excruciating where my elbow jammed into my gut as we made impact, and the air went out of my lungs. I crawled to a corner of the field and just laid there for a couple of hours. They checked me back into the Naval hospital. Later, I was diagnosed with a ruptured diaphragm in my left lung. They wanted to take out my spleen. Luckily, another doctor who actually knew what he was doing also examined me, and said the injury had nothing to do with my spleen. I just needed some "Darvon" (a narcotic pain reliever) and to get some rest for the next five days while they 'observed' me. That was the best rest that I had in all of boot camp. I missed the 'obstacle course' training because I was in the hospital recovering from the baseball incident. No problem. When I was released for the second time, they gave me a 'no physical, no drill' chit that allowed me to walk around the base instead of jogging everywhere, so I actually made out pretty well. Boot camp was almost over. I had lost my 'pitcher' position on the baseball team due to my second hospital stay. Again, I had no problem with that. It was early November. Instead, I volunteered for 'broad jump', jumping over 18 feet with oversized tennis shoes, and took first place out of the whole 800 guys in boot camp at the time. Everybody was surprised; even me. However, they didn't know that I had been the fastest guy on my track team in high school, which along with sprints, the 100-yard dash, the quarter-mile, the 880 relay, and mile relay, also included the 'long jump'. I jumped over 19 feet in high school. The black guys in my company were stunned at my success, but that didn't take away from the victory. Our company placed well in 'Sports week', partly as a result of my win. In the end, we marched, we graduated, and we went on leave at Christmas in December, with orders that subsequently took me to TI (California) in January, 1973 where I waited for further orders, and assignment to a ship.

So, it was March 1973, and I had been "in the Navy now" for about 6 months. It "wasn't a job, it was an adventure" according to the TV ad at the time. Boot Camp was behind me and we were in 'transit' at the Naval Air Base at TI (Treasure Island) near San Francisco, waiting to be assigned to a ship. Swabbing decks, playing spades. Waiting. Watching. Wet. It had been raining cats and dogs, and toads and frogs, for several weeks straight, for well over a month, with no let up. One of the sailors got the great idea to rent a car for the weekend and drive north from San Francisco to 'see the California coast'. There were three of us. We were scheduled to rotate out of TI the following week to someplace in Southeast Asia. We didn't know where. Neither did they. Ships move. So we were stuck in 'transit' waiting for our orders. A ride up the California coast sounded like fun.

Looose Ends

I want to be alone,
I mean really alone.
No family, no face,
no friends.

I want to be a stone,
a colorless stone,
no home, no ties,
loose ends!

I want to be free;
I mean really free!
No parties, no noise;
just quiet.
I want to be me, only lonely me.
I want to be free to try it.

I want to roam,
without a home,
to hike, or bike,
or thumb it.

To be a poem.
A lone Jerome.
I'd like to cleanly
bum it.

I want to blend,
and not pretend
to be something
I'm not.

I want to end,
and start again,
and see
just what I've got.

A colorless stone,
a buried bone,
an island, a cloud,
a sonnet.
On my own.
A pale tone.
a sail, airfoil,
or comet!

Jaak - 1973, South China Sea

7

UPSIDE DOWN

Illegitimi non carborundum ~ "Don't let the bastards grind you down".

Sanjo Casagrande headed south, down the highway toward Des Moines. The April sky was overcast with a hint of sun poking through the morning haze. Northbound traffic passed with headlights on, as Sanjo peered over the hood of his freshly washed red 'Ford 150' pick-up truck. He watched as reflections of the oncoming cars drove upside-down in his hood, flowing like raindrops to the port side, then disappeared over the edge of the hood as he drove. The images were funny, he thought, and entertaining; like watching a movie. He relaxed and let out a deep yawn, comforted by the swinging crucifix dangling from his rear- view mirror as he drove. He made a sign of the cross, recited a short prayer, asking God, Saint Christopher, and all angels and saints for safe travel. It felt good to be on the open road again, looking forward to a new adventure. A grey day, … but a good day for driving, he thought.

He had a late start after making phone calls in response to the morning e-mail. Initially, he had planned to leave his condo around 7:30 am to arrive in Des Moines by nightfall. He wanted to be sharp for his meeting the following morning, so wanted to leave the condo early. Burdened with thoughts about work, as well as his home life. Not heavy burdens, just, well, he had a lot on his mind. He was used to mulling over the details in his head to prevent problems. Of course, his family was also less stressed whenever Sanjo left town for a few days; so they felt at ease when he announced that he was taking a short business trip. It had been two hours since he left home, and therefore needed to make up some time.

He turned on the radio to catch the local news. He adjusted his seat to get more relaxed. He sipped some coffee that he had bought just ten minutes earlier while topping off his tank. A gallon of gas was now more than four bucks per gallon, and he felt better with a full tank. The economy was struggling with high unemployment, 45 million Americans were on food stamps, but Sanjo had a job. He felt settled, comfortable. Now he could think. The news drifted into the background as he listened to the same old tired stories that often made the American news. Another ball player was accused of murder, another of rape. A Bishop admitted that he had sex with a young boy, most of the people in Africa were dying of something, the Middle East was at war (again), a little girl was missing, and a domestic study showed that bacon and eggs are really good for us after all. And yes, today, global warming was again found to be a myth, they found life on Mars, and discovered that there was more oil in the western USA than all of the Middle Eastern countries combined. Soon, the voices on the radio gave way to the road noise as Sanjo only heard himself.

Sanjo liked to drive. When he drove, his mind wandered as he settled into the rhythm of the road and pondered the past. Decades ago he had been in the Navy, and he often thought of those timeless days at sea. Today as he drove, he began to question the purpose of the military. This was nothing new for Sanjo; he had questioned the military during his enlistment. So, it was just something that he did. Many years from now he thought, people would look back at war and wonder why they had fought over religion, territory, or a way of life after they were proven to be based upon faulty arguments and false propaganda. So, if war is fought in the name of Good versus Evil, who is good, and who is evil? It depends on one's perspective. Don't both sides essentially lose? What did the American Civil War actually accomplish? Aren't most wars fought over someone's belief or religion? Or, are wars merely fought by religious people who need oil? And, if so, is religion a good thing? Maybe religion too, is based on a faulty premise, like the benefits of bacon and eggs, Keynesian economics, a two party system of government, and the belief in global warming. Perhaps governments should stick to building roads. When all is said and done, what actually waits for us in the afterlife, a gay Bishop? When the gay Bishop stands up and rants that 'the meek shall inherit the earth', does he mean that the strong will survive, and they plan to just kill the weak and bury them in the earth? Although he believed in one God, he sensed that most people essentially worship the same God, even if they call their God by different names. Perhaps, he thought, he was a Nihilist. In fact, he liked the words of Albert Camus who wrote, *"I would rather live my life as if there is a God and die to find out there isn't, than live my life as if there isn't, and die to find out there is."* So he thought, and he questioned, and he resolved to find answers to his questions. Today, he decided, many things were upside-down.

Sanjo did not often look for inner-deeper-hidden meanings in life. But lately, he was giving a lot of thought to where he was, and where he was going. He was searching for meaning, and he was hungry for adventure. It was as much a philosophical journey as it was physical. He wanted answers to the questions; *What is life? Why am I here?* He decided that he would "Google" the name "Albert Camus" on Wikipedia when he checked into his hotel room for the evening.

He had been driving for more than two hours since his last stop, and he liked to pause every 150 miles or so to stretch, take a break, and fill the tank with gas. He was good for another two or three hours he thought. Sanjo began to fidget, and shifted in his seat. He decided to make a phone call to make sure that everything was set for the next day. Was there something he had missed? He picked up his cell phone and scrolled through the stored set of numbers to find his contact for tomorrow. Then, he pressed the "call" button. The phone rang and Randy Bidwell picked up.

"Hello, ... Randy Bidwell" the voice answered.

"Hi Randy. Sanjo Casagrande. How are you?" He asked. "I'm good Sanjo, wha's up?"

"Well, I'm on the road, and just calling to check that we're all set for tomorrow's meeting".

"Tomorrow's meeting? Randy asked. "I thought we scheduled the meeting for next Tuesday. That's what I wrote in my planner."

"Well it's been two weeks since we set it up, but I'm pretty sure that we agreed to meet tomorrow, Tuesday, the 13th" replied Sanjo.

"You know, you may be correct Sanjo. Let me check!" A short pause, then, "I had it planned for the 20th, and that's what I wrote in the e-mail that I sent to everyone in the office. Can we change it to a week from tomorrow?

"Well, I've been driving for a couple of hours Randy, but it's not too late to turn around. I'll plan for next Tuesday instead if that works better.

Tuesday the 20th, then".

"I'll do that Sanjo. Actually we're all set for next Tuesday. Sorry for the confusion"

"No problem" said Sanjo.

"OK then. Have a good weekend". "You too, Sanjo. Sorry".

"Well that's wonderful!" he muttered. "Now what?" he asked aloud.

"I'm all packed and headed south. Do I really want to return to Duluth? Maybe it's time for a holiday", he thought. I'll just keep heading south and perhaps make some cold calls in Iowa until next Tuesday. I'll call home and explain that there was a mix-up in communication and I have to spend the weekend in Des Moines and meet next Tuesday instead. In fact, maybe I'll just head down to Topeka and look up my old steaming buddy, Dick Redhouse. He moved to Kansas a few years back after he lost his construction job. We can catch up on old times and check out the top "tourist" traps. What's it been, 20 years or more? Yeah. I'll just keep driving, he decided. Ten minutes later, he pulled off the expressway into a rest area to study the map. He found that he could still head south, pick up I-35 South to Kansas City, then I-70 West to Topeka. All right then! To Topeka it is! *Goin' to Kansas City, … Kansas City here I come ….* He took the next exit off the E-way and drove down a back road off the service drive, then stepped out of his truck to stretch his legs, relieve his bladder, and stretch his arms and back. Then, he hopped back into his pickup and made his way back onto the expressway, and continued south. The sky was beginning to clear and the road was dry. It's a good day for a drive, he reasoned. As he drove south, he remembered a poem that his pal 'Redhouse' had written many years earlier;

Real-eyes

Nothing is real,
It's just what we make it.
We're making the motions,
While we really just fake it.

They feed us the data,
and like fools we take it'.
Trying to expand our mind;
Instead we just bake it.

When will it end,
This follow the leader?

Sanjo didn't know whether it was because Redhouse had repeated the poem so often, or because he had subconsciously repeated the poem to himself, .. but at long last, the words began to sink in, and made sense. *"Nothing is real, It's just what we make it. We're making the motions, while we really just fake it."* he thought to himself. Was it that his own reality was something that was contrived, and he just chose to believe it as fact? Are we as a people, brainwashed to believe the many memes, that others believe to be reality, … and those beliefs became our reality? Maybe he was just reading too much into it. As an old English professor had long ago advised, *"Don't look for inner-deeper-hidden meanings, it will just make everything more complicated"*. On the other hand, could he teach himself to believe in another reality, and thus change the way he thought entirely? Maybe so! *"Trying to expand our mind. When will it end, this follow the leader?* Sanjo vowed that he would research the subject of "quantum jumping" sometime during his current 'holiday' road trip, to explore new realities, and possibly gain a better perspective of his existence. In an upside down world, Sanjo decided that he needed to put his own world right side up.

MY SHIP

Upon arrival back at the Naval Air base in San Francisco we had only a few days wait until we received our new orders. I was assigned to the USS Flint, AE-32, an ammunition ship. I flew from San Francisco to Clark Air Base in Manila, then made my way over to Subic Bay Naval Air station, near Olongapo, Philippines, three hours by bus, after a short stay in California. I was still recovering from the car wreck, but we didn't report the accident to the people in the Navy. What was the point? We had filed a police report with the local sheriff in northern California, so we thought we were covered. There had been three of us on the little journey, but the third guy had been sleeping back at the hotel when the crash occurred, and only showed up after the wreck. Although, 'The sleeper' was the one who took the rap, since he carried the insurance. The other two guys suffered no injuries. So we let the whole ordeal slide. Again, I had to wait. My ship was still somewhere in the South China Sea, off the coast of Vietnam, and I would have to wait until it reached port. They didn't know which port. So I waited.

They had all the 'transit' guys situated in a little prison camp with barbed wire fences and covered wooden guard towers in each corner like you might see in some old World War II movie with Steve McQueen, to keep us safe (I guess). Every day we mustered on deck at 6 AM, had breakfast in the camp galley, then, policed the grounds to pick up any garbage lying around. They tried to keep us busy. We played football to pass the time, and went into Olongapo on liberty at night when they were good enough to let us out of the camp. We were all in transit waiting to be shipped or flown to other destinations to meet our ships. I spent about a month in the prison camp until one day I received my orders to catch a commercial flight out of Manila to Taipei, Taiwan with one overnight stay, then on to Kaohsiung, Taiwan to meet my ship.

Upon arriving in Kaohsiung, I was taken to the place where my ship was supposed to be, only to find that they don't often allow US Navy ammunition ships to come into foreign ports because they have a history of exploding, thus causing a lot of destruction. The USS Flint (AE 32) was anchored a few miles out from the mainland, and had just returned from 'The Line' in Vietnam where they had been resupplying other ships with bombs and bullets. They were now in the Kaohsiung area to restock the ship with ammo and enjoy a week of R&R.

I took a local water taxi out to the ship to report for duty. When I arrived at the ship anchored out at sea, I climbed the accommodation ladder to the quarterdeck and requested "permission to come aboard" as we were trained to do. But there was practically nobody on board. It was like a ghost ship. A sailor took me to the 'M Division' berthing compartment in the aft part of the ship located below the flight deck, and above the main shaft, where I was assigned a locker and a temporary rack. Then someone told me to go ashore and join the party. Only watch standers and critical crew members remained on board for the most part.

The ship's captain at the time had rented the 'Hotel Kennedy' in Kaohsiung for a little R&R, and week-long ship's party, to show support for the crew. It was early 1973. The Captain could do that with his high rank, as he was one of the more senior captains in the US Navy at the time. He was a good captain. In any case, we partied for the rest of the week at the Kennedy, then, everyone returned to the ship. Things got interesting after that. We restocked with 'bombs and bullets' in Kaohsiung, then headed back to 'the line' for 'Operation Endsweep'; a mine clearing operation off the coast of Vietnam, for which we all received additional 'hazardous duty' pay as part of a battle group. I had learned a few things in my first Asian 'Party Port' with a bunch of drunken sailors, followed by the rigorous routine of working sixteen to twenty hour days at sea as a Machinist Mate aboard a US Navy ship. Our mission was to resupply destroyers, aircraft carriers, frigates, and other ships from dawn 'til dusk with bombs, bullets, oil, jet fuel, and other supplies on a continued basis. I tried to keep everyone cool by making sure the air conditioning and refrigeration systems kept working along with my other tasks. Along with sailors, we had Navy Seals, marines, and divers on board that were experienced in UD (underwater demolition), as well as mine countermeasure. Constant fire drills, spot inspections, and general quarters for eight to ten hours at a time at our battle stations, as well as watches while underway that were '4 and 8'. Four hours on, with eight hours off between watches; which meant that besides our other routine maintenance to fix everything that was breaking, or might break (Planned Maintenance System, PMS) for equipment listed in DC Central (Damage Control), we stood four hour watches between eight hour breaks, while working up to sixteen hours per day.

At sea, we would 'Vertrep' or 'Unrep', which was short for 'Vertical Replenishment' and 'Underway Replenishment'. In the first case, we used two onboard (CH-46, Sea Knight) helicopters to pick up pallets of ammo from our flight deck with Huey helicopters (helos) and place the cargo aboard a ship steaming alongside at several knots, not more than 50 yards away. In the case of 'Underway Replenishment' we would shoot a line across to the other ship, then pass pallets of ammo while steaming alongside. Many times we had ships on both the starboard and port sides connected by lines to our ship being resupplied with the onboard winches for several hours. It was a dangerous operation, every time. Occasionally, we would have a smaller Navy Destroyer on one side of the ship, with an Aircraft Carrier on the other side, working both sides. When we eventually broke away after a couple hours of replenishment, we would play our 'Breakaway Song', the 'Orange Blossom Special' over the Flint's loudspeaker system. Always a treat.

We also had two flags that we flew during replenishment operations for the USS Flint (AE 32). One with a picture of 'Fred Flintstone' that read 'The Bedrock Bullet Company', and another flag with a picture of 'Barney Rubble' that read 'You Call, We Haul'.

https://www.youtube.com/watch?v=9f_QySKfsgI

USS Flint (AE-32) Fred Flintstone, The Bedrock Bullet Company

USS Flint (AE-32) Barney Rubble, You Call, We Haul

THE LINE

*Below the surface of the water, underneath reflected sky, I
watched the morning twilight as the star lights floated by.*
- Watchstander

*Richard Redhouse had been drifting again. It had been over 30 years since
he had been discharged from the Navy, and he still couldn't get that ship out of
his head. After so many years, he could still walk the passageways, and stand
on the flying bridge watching the waves crash over the bow. He could stand
in the hanger bay and watch the helo's land on the flight deck as they brought
the daily bags of mail back from Saigon. He could smell the mixture of diesel
fuel, paint, and bilge water in the engine room, smell the steam, and turn the
valve handles on the condenser water bypass valve. And, he could hear Chief
Grunhaus bark "If it moves, salute it! If doesn't, paint it! As he walked the ship,
he could talk to the "buds" still on board, because they never changed their
appearance or behavior from his memory of them long ago.*

*It seemed like yesterday. To Richard Redhouse and the "buds", it really
wasn't just a job, but truly a great adventure.*

MM3 Redhouse stood on the flying bridge looking out over the fo'c'sle,
past the bow of the ship as they made their way west toward the Gulf of
Aden. On this particular cruise he had just come off watch about an hour
before, and he enjoyed gazing out over the ocean in the early hours of the
morning. The ship heaved and yawed in harmonic, hypnotic motion as it
pushed its way through the warm waters of the Indian Ocean, displacing
several thousand tons of water as it moved. He could hear the water gush
and gurgle along the hull, and watch the waves roll away as dolphins raced
along the starboard side, playing in the wake as they leaped from wave to
wave. Bracing himself against the bulkhead, he could feel the hard gray

painted steel, and the vibrations of the ship through his boondockers. The oscillations seemed to penetrate his boots and move all the way up to his head, as he felt the energy and force of the large mass pushing its way west. Looking to starboard, he estimated that they were making about 15 knots. It was a clear morning with a slight wind. The sea was blue-green with a few distant white-tipped waves, ... yet the breeze was warm. The sky was mostly sunny with a few low-hanging clouds that were reflected as dark areas on the water. The clouds were low over the water, ... some just 50 feet off the surface. The "three inch fifties" above the main deck pointed straight ahead and made it plain to see that this was not a cruise ship. He could see a destroyer on the horizon to the northeast and he knew that they were not alone. Then, the voice over the 1MC loudspeaker crackled "Turn to! Commence ships work!" and Redhouse went below.

He could smell the fresh brewed coffee coming up through the hatch as he descended the ladder heading aft toward the filter cleaning shop. Several sailors passed him on the way to their duty stations on the command "turn to".

"Morning Redhouse!" said Henderson. "Morning Henderson" replied Redhouse. "Was' happenin' Redhouse?" asked Jones. "Hey Jones!" said Richard.

"Kiss my rosy red ass" said Engineman Bradley. "Eat me, Bradley! Replied Redhouse.

And so it went, on down the passageway, past the after-berthing compartment below the flight deck, through two more hatched doorways into the filter- cleaning shop.

They had just finished the morning muster on the flight deck. The "buds" were already gathered, waiting to divide their planned maintenance assignments for the morning. Most of the sailors held a mug of coffee in their hands (a cup of Joe, as it's called in the Navy) as they sat on anything that would support them. HT2 "Crazy Joe" Melnik sat with his feet up on the stainless steel sink counter. Fireman Jake Freeman sat in the corner on the handle of a vacuum pump. MM3 Billy Ortega pulled up a refrigeration compressor that he had pulled from service. Fireman "Bad Bob" Seaman sat on the deck with his legs crossed and his back against the bulkhead. EN3 Ernie Bern entered the space and pulled up a chair in the corner next to the storage locker. This was their third week out of Singapore after battling 30 foot seas through the Straits of Malacca near Thailand and they were well into their daily routines.

Crazy Joe broke the silence.

"Hey, did you guys see the UFO's floating over the horizon yesterday around sunset?"

"There were about six of 'em. Just sat there in the sky like dancing orbs,.. balls of light, sort of bobbing up and down on the horizon like steel balls in a pachinko game".

"We watched them for about five minutes, then wham! They shot off into space and disappeared in a split second, … and they were gone! Freaky!"

Jake Freeman cut in. "When you say 'We', what you mean 'we' Kimosabe?" "I mean "We" said Melnik. "Redhouse was with me. He'd never seen them before."

"Were you stoned?" asked Bad Bob.

"No, straight as your pecker in the California Club. I've seen them before too!"

Henderson was a bit skeptical. "How do you know they were flying saucers?" "They weren't saucers really" said Melnik. "They looked more like shiny balls of silver and light. They changed colors and danced around". "How far away were they? asked Engineman Bern.

"That's hard to say. Maybe a mile or two. Maybe less. I'm not sure. They were quite a ways off, and it's hard to tell their size, so I'm not sure how far they were. But, we could see them clearly enough."

"I'll say this, … they were not from this world. We don't make anything that can hover like that, … then shoot off into space and disappear that fast."

"Just look to the sky whenever you get above deck, and someday you'll see them too!" promised Melnik. It was broad daylight when we saw them!

After some additional discussion, the men divided up their maintenance chores, then headed off to carry out their assigned tasks.

Redhouse went back above to the main deck to breathe some fresh ocean air. He had met the ship in Kaohsiung, Taiwan a year earlier on his first WESPAC cruise to the South China Sea. This was his second cruise, so by now he felt as if he had been in the Navy his entire life. He had mixed feelings about the Navy, but he very much enjoyed being at sea despite the long days and endless work. The ship's motto was *Judicemur Agendo*, which meant, "let us be judged by our actions" and seemed like a good place to be at this juncture in his life, as he tried to figure out how to best position himself for the future. The economy back in the states was in a downturn anyway in the early '70's, so the Navy was an interim move. As the wind picked up a bit, the misty salt air of the ocean breeze speckled his new beard, and mixed with the smell of diesel fuel and fresh paint to bring a sense of realism to the notion that he was in fact "in the Navy now".

The crew had earlier spent a well-earned week in port losing their pay to the local bars, street hustlers, and "hostesses" who made their living by haranguing any passing group of sailors, marines, or tourists that crossed their paths. Now short of cash, the crew was content to "turn to", resume their duties, and succumb to their fates while suffering with their new tattoos, and long lines to sickbay for shots of amoxicillin. Henderson was somewhat embarrassed about the new image of *Mighty Mouse* charging skyward from his belly button, but big Billy Blahnik the BT was quite proud of his tattoo that just read "Your Name" that was stamped prominently on his ass.

In the Navy, there were sailors from every city, town, village, and burg in America, as well as a few Filipinos that usually worked as "deck-apes", or cooks on the mess decks. Redhouse learned early on that he was going to have to re- think his previously held concepts of how the world worked if he was going to get along. If America is a melting pot, then the Navy is clam chowder. With that said, every sailor on the ship was just another clam swimming in the soup, putting in their time.

Petty Officer Redhouse was a practical sort of guy, with a good sense of humor and an easy smile. He came from the Midwest like many of his pals on board. He was surprised at the number of shipmates that came from farms and small towns in the Midwest, who had never actually seen the ocean before joining the Navy. Many of his "snipe" friends were from Nebraska, South Dakota, Iowa, Minnesota, Illinois, Michigan, Indiana, and Wisconsin. Redhouse came from a small town in Minnesota. It probably helped that he was also a bit of a con man by nature and pretty good at sizing up the people he met. At 5' 10", with straight shoulders, dirty blond hair, and a slender frame, he could not be considered a big man, but he could hold his own if called upon. He was quick, had a keen eye, and a solid demeanor that served him well. He carried himself with confidence without being too brash. In other words, he was typical of the rest of the guys in the engineering group. He was a mechanic. His lucky number was four. And he believed that everything in life could be related to football, cars, and craps.

Redhouse was a mechanic, but also somewhat of a poet. It wasn't that he was especially adept at putting machinery together or taking it apart. Quite the opposite; he didn't really like smashing his knuckles or getting his hands so black that it took a week's work and a pound of soap to remove the grime from beneath his fingernails. He had worked in a few construction jobs prior to enlisting, so he was good with his hands, … but he was only semi-skilled. He was a sort of mastermind, but surely, more of a philosopher than a mechanic. The guy who could put it all together, mix it up, and deliver the fine-tuned plan. Then, when the plan was clear, he could execute it. He was a natural. He was a bit skewed, a bit out of his element as a Machinist Mate assigned to "A gang" aboard the ship, and he worked on a variety of equipment, and general maintenance assignments, whether the ship was underway or in port.

Along with being good with his hands, he had an easy way with people. He was able to reach consensus without grinding people the wrong way. He had a sort of self-assured *savoir-faire*. When he would get upset or agitated he would just say, in a mid-west sort of way, "That really grinds my beans!" And that was that. He could make everyone in the group feel important, like everything they said was their own idea, like *they* were the masterminds. At 23, he was a bit older than his colleagues who were one or two years younger, but with his innocent grin and constrained confidence, he fit in well with just about any group that he joined. They called him the "old man" and he wore the handle well. When Dick ran the plan, everything worked like a well-greased rail.

Nevertheless, not every idea went according to plan. So, as they steamed toward the line, their minds were often focused on "steaming" in the next party port of call. And one of their favorite ports was Olongapo, in the Philippines, with its mile stretch of bars on both sides of the main street, and a steady stream of sailors heading toward the *California Club* after too many sober weeks at sea.

Watchstander

The ocean was as ruffled silk,
The night air, clear and still.
The moon sat like a beacon
in the quiet morning chill.

Clouds sailed by before it,
Partly covering its face,
As I stared across the water
through the dimly lighted space.

Enveloped in morning mist,
I watched the morning moon.
The last hours of the watch,
And the Sun would be up soon.

The sky was looking brighter,
partly cloudy in the East.
The daylight was approaching,
the wind had almost ceased.

Below the surface of the water,
Underneath reflected sky,
I watched the morning twilight
as the star lights floated by.

Grey cotton clouds hung in the air,
Underneath the blue,
Orange horseshoe of horizon,
Complementary hue.

The blending of the morning
Overtakes the night.
It's show time every sunrise
With the ever-changing light.

The minutes passing faster
while my mind was at a rest,
on the last minutes of the watch
as I sat as mornings guest.

How happy is the watch stander
At quiet times like this.
"It's almost worth the hassle",
I said, in playful jest.

Jaak, - somewhere in the Indian
Ocean, 1974

Indian Ocean from the Flight Deck, 1974

Indian Ocean and 3"/ 50 Caliber Guns, 1974

THE CALIFORNIA CLUB

*"Ah, mon cher, for anyone who is alone, without God and
without a master, the weight of days is dreadful".*
- Albert Camus

Looking back, Sanjo couldn't recall whether "Cassandra" looked pretty to him or not when their eyes first met. As a "hostess" working in the *California Club*, she looked much like the other Filipino girls that worked the bars that lined both sides of the main street in Olongapo. Her real name was Marissa Marikit, but she took the name "Cassandra" when she began working in the clubs. The road past the main gate of the Naval base was blacktop with dirt shoulders in the 60's and 70's, and many of the back streets off the main drag were dirt and mud. The main street was a mile-long stretch of bars on both sides of the strip, with 13,000 'registered hostesses' in the clubs, and people dodging Jeepneys that constantly raced up and down the strip at a frenetic pace. A jeepney ride along the strip typically cost 10 to 25 centavos depending on the distance traveled. You could walk or ride depending on whether you were in a hurry, wanted to shop, or just felt lazy. Past the main gate, the culture changed from the regimented world of a military base and sea duty to a more chaotic, noisy, and frenzied pace that reminded Redhouse of a scene from the Wild West. From the moment they crossed the "Shit River" that sat directly outside the main gate of the Subic Bay Naval base, and entered Olongapo, their world changed.

Little Filipino kids would often gather next to the Shit River bridge yelling "Hey Joe, throw me coin", begging for money, then diving into the rancid river whenever someone tossed a few centavos. The smell of raw sewage hung heavy in the tropical air, and mixed with the sweeter smell of the Pacific island vegetation as they crossed the bridge on their march to the clubs. Many of the girls looked rather exotic to a bunch of eager sailors and marines entering uncontrolled territory for the first time. Especially since, the Filipino girls didn't look like "home town" girls, and the sailors became more intoxicated as they advanced. It was also apparent that over the past couple of hundred years or so, the Philippines had been occupied at one time or another by Spanish, American, Japanese, and perhaps even a few Frenchmen along the way; so the girls came from a diverse gene pool. Overall, "Cassandra" was one of the more alluring girls, and one of the best dancers; but really, they all looked good to a bunch of sex seeking, not-so-sober sailors.

Crazy Joe Melnik, Dick Redhouse, and Sanjo too, all loved Olongapo and the girls along the strip. On this occasion, there were several ships in port at Subic Bay, since they were all there to take on stores and resupply for the next mission in the South China Sea. So they often saw their old shipmates, as well as familiar faces and crews from other ships as they toured the back streets of Olongapo. It was like 'old home week' in the islands. The Philippines just had a different feel to it than other ports like Kaohsiung (Taiwan), Yokosuka (Japan), Sattahip (Thailand) or Hong Kong. There was more of a sedated South Pacific island appeal to the place, unlike the more "crowded city" feel of some of the other Southeast Asian ports. The different ships all operated in the same South Pacific theater, so not only would the sailors see familiar faces in the various ports, they would also see the various ships at sea during their individual missions as the ships were steaming alongside, or as they would 'breakaway' after an UNREP exercise. So, in port they could put the faces together with the various ships that were working in the same area, on similar missions. The weather was usually hot and sunny with hundreds of palm trees swaying in the warm dry breeze. When they landed in Olongapo, and passed through the main gates, it felt like it was time to party. And so they did, as they proceeded to explore every bar on the strip, with the abundant Filipino bands blasting a wide variety of "hit tune" music onto the streets, until they finally made their way to the *California Club*.

"Hey Joe, I love you no shit, you buy me drink?" came a cry from the group of girls that greeted every sailor entering their bar.

"I love you no shit, buy your own (expletive) drink" jeered Melnik.

"Hey Joe, wha' sheep you on?" "Wha's you name?" the girls persisted with the same questions to each of the sailors in their squeaky little Filipino voices, mocking the sailors stumbling through the entryway, with their eyes trying to adjust to the distant corners of the bar to identify the best looking "hostesses".

"Bill, .. my name is Bill" one of them lied. "Oh, …I like you Beeel", one of the girls said.

"Bring me a San Miguel" ordered another sailor.

"And a pitcher of Mojo" called another. And so they entered the darkened den. Petty Officer Melnik put his arm around one of the girls standing just inside the bar, and Cassandra just smiled and said "Hey Joe, .. You Butterfly, I cut you!", and Crazy Joe dropped his arm.

Cassandra was Crazy Joe Melnik's favorite girl. Crazy Joe would make his way down the strip to the California Club whenever he was in Olongapo. Because the club was about half way down the strip, Joe would make a few stops at some of the other bars before he got to the club. This made Cassandra appear even better to Joe by the time he arrived. But Cassandra always knew that Joe had stopped at the other bars earlier because of the great communication between the girls on the strip, … each of them knowing which girl had been with which sailor, and which bars they had frequented before. That's why Cassandra accused Joe of being a "Butterfly" for flitting between her and the other girls on the strip. Because Frank Valero was one of Crazy Joe's steaming buddies, he and a few other snipes would also make their way down the strip, stopping by to see other girl friends as they went. So, when it was Frank's turn to go on Liberty, and while Crazy Joe was standing watch that evening back aboard the ship, Frank would also stop in and see Cassandra. Frank became almost as familiar with Cassandra as Crazy Joe. And, they all liked the way that Cassandra danced. The truth is that Cassandra favored Frank over Crazy Joe, but never let on that she favored one sailor over another. The odd thing was that Crazy Joe couldn't get Cassandra out of his mind. It seemed as if she was all that Joe could think about every time the ship got underway, and his anxiety level would increase each time the ship completed a mission, then turned around to return to Olongapo to load new supplies. Sanjo liked Cassandra too, and would look her up when his ship was in port. So, all the buds not only shared the same missions, they also shared the same favorite girls when their particular ship happened to be in that port. They all liked Cassandra, but they also liked Alice, Carlotta, Virgie, Amy, Ruby, Mila, Marina, and many of the other strippers. So, perhaps it was just destiny, or maybe serendipity, that Sanjo had a very warm fondness for Cassandra as well. Sanjo Casagrande was off another ammunition ship that had pulled into one of the other berthing spots at the pier, as they often did to resupply prior to the next deployment. Sometimes, there were three, four, or five ships in port at the same time, and Redhouse and Crazy Joe knew a few of the sailors from the other ships from previous deployments or ship transfers.

In any case, they often addressed each other by their last name, since that's the way they were addressed in the Navy by the officers and chiefs. So Frank was just 'Valero', and Richard was 'Redhouse', and Sanjo was 'Casagrande'. One thing that Redhouse detested was being called "Dick", and although he thought it condescending to be called by his last name, he thought it was more demeaning to be called by his first name. He preferred the name "Redhouse", or Machinist Mate Redhouse, or Petty Officer Redhouse. They had a nice ring, he thought. That's what officers and chiefs called him anyway. *Maybe I should just change my name to 'Jack'*, he thought, when he bumped into Frank Valero in Olongapo, the day that Frank left town for the last time. Only a few of his close friends called him by his first name, and they usually called him Dick. HT2 Frank Valero was one of them.

The last time that Redhouse had seen Valero was two nights earlier in the *California Club*, on the main drag a half-mile into town. Frank was falling all over his little friend Yolanda while she was sucking up to a few of his shipmates. It was their third night back in port after spending two months on "the line". They were an hour from curfew and all of them were falling-down drunk. Frank sat at a table near the bar with a collection of empty *San Miguel* beer bottles and a half-empty pitcher of "Mojo" in front of him. He was again announcing his plans to marry Yolanda when he returned to the States, while his "buds" were trying to talk some sense into him. Sitting at a table alongside Frank were Danny Dougherty from Detroit, "Crazy Joe" Melnik from Sioux City, Iowa, Billy Blahnik from McCook, Nebraska, "Skippy" Ortega from Albuquerque, New Mexico, and a group of Crazy Joe's big bohemian BT buddies. Engineman Ernie

Bern from Wyoming was leaning against the bar. They had just had their picture taken by a local bar photographer because it was Ortega's birthday and they wanted a picture with their "girls" for posterity. The way the other guys saw it, Yolanda was just another little "I love you no sheet, you buy me drink" bar girl who would hit on any sea-legged sailor that walked into her malodorous little bar. A few of them were trying to talk Frank into saving his money for the new Jeep he wanted to buy when he returned to port in San Francisco. But Frank wouldn't hear any of it. Many months later, Yolanda eventually did turn up in New Orleans, and Frank also bought the jeep. While Joe Melnik bought a gold neck chain with a charm in the shape of a heart that just read "I love you no shit, buy your own f##kin' drink".

That night began with BT2 Billy Blahnik walking up to the first Marine that he found in the bar, then betting him five bucks that he had his name tattooed on his ass. When the Marine fell for the ploy, Blahnik pulled down his trousers to reveal the words *Your Name* tattooed in big letters on his right butt cheek, then bought a round for the house with his winnings. The night ended with BT2 Billy Blahnik hitting Machinist Mate Ortega over the head with a beer bottle for drinking the last San Miguel beer, while everyone ran for the exits when the shore patrol arrived. Ortega had to be taken to sickbay to get six stitches put in his forehead. That also ended the party since there was a curfew in place and everyone had to be off the streets by midnight. So, it was either back to the ship, or pick a girl and head to her place for the evening. Joe Melnik and Sanjo Casagrande decided to catch one of the last jeepneys back to the main gate, and take the long walk back to their respective ships to sleep off the night's damage in their own racks, and catch breakfast the next morning, before the morning muster. Redhouse ended up heading back to Cassandra's place somewhere in Olongapo to sleep off the "Mojo" and enjoy her companionship.

At the time, she lived in a tidy little two room mud stucco "casa" with dirt floors, and barred openings in the wall where windows should have been, no indoor plumbing, but with a comfortable little bed and a pink electric fan to circulate the air next to the bed. A metal pot sat in the corner in case someone had to "use the bathroom". The way that worked was that one would squat over the pot and do their business, then throw the contents out the opening that was the window, where it would then run down into the street and be carried off through a ditch back to the shit river. The only distraction was that someone's grandparents slept in the adjacent room on a rug on the dirt floor, with only some hanging beads in the doorway to separate the rooms, while she and her sailor friend got the bed because it paid better. In the morning Redhouse would awake to roosters crowing beginning at sun-up around 4:00 am, which didn't help his hangover. The crowing would last for about an hour. Redhouse would then roll out of bed and urinate outside next to the building before heading back to the ship for morning muster on the flight deck when the main gates opened before 6:00 am. Sometime over the next few days, after they got underway again, he wrote a poem entitled "*Olongapo*" to help him later recall that experience.

A few weeks after their *California Club* rendezvous, Dick Redhouse was back in Olongapo after spending the night in town again. He was walking back to the base near the bus station when he heard a familiar voice call his name.

"Hey Dick!" yelled Frank from across the street. "I see you survived the night!"

"Yeah! I spent the night in town after the bars closed, rather than stay on the streets after curfew" Redhouse responded.

"I didn't see you at quarters. Are you UA?" asked Frank.

"No. Grunhaus gave me special liberty to pick up some dungarees and dress whites at the laundry, so I just stayed in town" said Redhouse.

"OK, I understand. I saw you outside the main gate earlier, so I grabbed a jeepney to say good-bye" said Frank. "I'm heading over to Clark airbase in Manila in about half-an-hour to return to the States". I have orders to return to Treasure Island. What's that in your pocket, or are you just glad to see me?"

Redhouse reached down in his pocket and pulled out a wrinkled sheet of paper with some notes written on both sides and handed it to Frank.

"I wrote a few lines to remind me of the past couple of days in port" said Redhouse.

"Not another poem!" said Frank.

"Yeah, I wrote it yesterday, .. see what you think!"

"I'll read it on the bus!" said Frank. "I have to catch a '*Victory Liner*' to Clark.

I'm on my way over to the bus station now".

"OK" said Redhouse. "Have a safe flight back to TI. I'll catch up with you back in California."

In those days, Olongapo had many dirt streets off the main strip that would turn into a river of mud when the rains came. During the 60's and 70's, it was a staging point for troops, supplies, and services to support the war effort and the US Navy "WesPac" 7th fleet in the South Pacific. The Supply Depot in Subic Bay, Republic of the Philippines, included the Cubi Point Naval Air Station in Subic Bay, as well as ship repair facilities, piers for US Navy ships, warehouses, offices, and barracks for thousands of Sailors, Marines, Construction Battalions, Navy Seals, and other government and civilian personnel. The Air Force guys were located at Clark Air Base near Manila about three or four hours away by bus (depending on which roads were traveled). Clark is where they flew out of the Philippines to return to the "country".

The Subic Bay Naval base had a couple of bowling alleys, a movie theater, a PX where military personnel bought their stereo equipment, golf courses, riding stables, restaurants, and its own bars for enlisted personnel and another one for the officers. The sailors could also bring their girlfriends from town onto the base, as long as they escorted them. However, it was actually more fun to go into Olongapo to meet the girls, than to bring the girls onto the base. Nevertheless, they occasionally conceded to bringing their favorite girls to the bars on the base if they requested. Olongapo, situated just outside of the main gates of the Navy base and across the Shit River, was a town that consisted of a mile long stretch of bars with about 13,000 registered "hostesses" that serviced the troops. On a typical night in Olongapo, especially when a carrier came into port, there was a 'shit load' of activity. Shore patrols and "green-hats", the special police units, cruised the streets every night breaking up fights between sailors, marines, and anyone else that might be in the way, who could always be found rolling around in the mud and dirt, and busting up the bars with each other. But then, … what would you expect. The paddy wagons were always the busiest as the midnight curfew approached. But on many nights, the shore patrol units consisted of the same shipmates standing shore patrol duty instead of standing watch aboard the ships. So, one night the sailors would drink, and get picked up by the shore patrol for being drunk and disorderly, .. and the following night they would pick up their other shipmates while they themselves stood Shore Patrol duty, as their shipmates staggered out of the bars in the same condition that they had been in the night before.

As Frank stepped aboard the bus, the marquis read "VICTORY LINER 504". He thought "what an odd name for a bus!" He remembered a sign that was mounted on a bulkhead above an engine room ladder on an ocean-going tug that read, *you can't make footprints in the sands of time, while sitting on your ass!* That's what he was thinking as he sat down to endure the four hour bus ride down bumpy jungle roads, and past rice fields with water buffaloes through the Philippine countryside, from Subic Bay to Clark Air Base, after leaving the ship for the last time. He chose a seat near the middle of the bus, swung his sea bag into the overhead rack, then took out the wrinkled sheet of paper that Redhouse had handed him in town. It was a poem entitled simply '*Olongapo*' that Redhouse had written about his night with Cassandra during their earlier sojourn in the Philippine port. Apparently, Redhouse hadn't made it back to the ship like he had said. He read the poem and chuckled, thinking that Redhouse had a way with words. The poem pretty much described what Frank thought about the place as well. Although, that wasn't entirely true. He also had a strong attachment to the town in other ways. After he finished reading Dick's poem, he reached into another pocket and pulled out a letter from Cassandra explaining to Frank that she was pregnant, and thought that Frank could very well be the father of her child. This became a significant concern to Frank, but what could he do, he wondered? He was on his way back to California, leaving Olongapo, Cassandra, and the *California Club* behind. Nevertheless, it gave Frank a lot to think about as he made the long bus trip through the rice fields and jungle to Manila. 'Yesterday's history, tomorrow's a mystery", he thought. Besides that, what made her think that Frank was the father, when she had been with so many other guys? He would have to get back in touch with Cassandra later.

That was the last time that Frank Valero had seen Redhouse, until about 20 years later. Frank went to work for a shipbuilder somewhere on the US Gulf Coast after he was discharged from the Navy. Over the course of the next couple of decades, they would occasionally correspond via Christmas cards with a few short notes, but he never did write Cassandra back to discover the outcome of her conundrum. Frank liked the poems that Redhouse wrote, and he encouraged Redhouse to publish them. To prompt him to publish the poems, Frank would sometimes write in the Christmas cards, *"you can't make footprints in the sands of time, while sitting on your ass!"*. But Redhouse never acknowledged his taunts.

During his three WesPac tours while in the Navy, it was rumored that approximately 150 sailors from his ship alone had married Filipino and Asian girls. And, the full complement of enlisted personnel and officers only consisted of about 350 enlisted men and officers aboard the ship during each deployment. That spoke volumes about the girls from places like the *California Club*. The town of Olongapo still exists today, but in a somewhat different form from the "Wild West" days of the 60's and 70's when many of the roads were dirt or mud and the street stretched for a mile down the main road with mostly bars on both sides of the street, and jeepneys kicked up dust as they raced up and down the strip. They had paved the main roads with cement by 1975 during Redhouse's last deployment, and the place never felt the same again. Both Clark Airbase and Olongapo were buried in ash when Mount Pinatubo erupted in the Philippines in June of 1991, after the Navy pulled out of Subic Bay for good. But that was long after the Viet Nam war had ended in 1975. Nevertheless, the memories, the girls, and probably a few orphans remained as a result of the military involvement there. Casagrande, Redhouse, and Valero all felt nostalgia for their favorite party port. And to the present day, they all still felt a fondness for Cassandra; A wonderful dancer, and stripper 'par excellence'.

Olongapo

I'm bunked down drunk,
my stomach's in knots.
I got a PI honey, and the GI trots.
It's been eight long hours since I took the ride
From the shipboard boogie, to the other side.

I feel hung over
With the roosters crowin'
soundin' reveille loud as bugles blowin'.
I'd feel much better where there's no one 'round,
to hear the beatin' 'tween my eardrums pound.
In a quiet little corner where there's no more sound,
while my head's goin' through the lost and found.

The body next to me is brown,
but all I can manage is a gaseous frown,
'cause a high ain't nothin' when you're comin' down
from a night long cruise in a party town
When all you got left is an empty head,
And your honey's got your money And she looks half dead.
All you can do is hold your bed
and try to forget the things you've said.

But if I had it all to do over again,
I'd do it all the same.
When there's no one 'round to tuck you in at night
There's no one 'round to blame.

And I'm gonna quit drinkin'
And give up my smoke
After one more drink,
and one more toke.
I'm serious now! That ain't no joke!
I must be half insane.

Jaak - Off the Philippine coast, 1974

A Horse and Buggy, Olongapo, Philippines, 1973

Victory Liner stopping by the Milky Way, Philippines, 1974

THE HAMPTONS

'Of all the gin joints, in all the towns, in all the world, she walks into mine' - Casablanca

While heading down the expressway toward Kansas, Sanjo reached down with his right hand to feel his rucksack sitting on the floor next to him to make sure that he had his laptop with him. Then, he turned off the I-35 exit ramp towards the Hampton Inn that he had reserved for the night near Des Moines. It began to drizzle, and he could see dark clouds blowing in from the West. The song playing on the radio was *"Thunderstorms and Neon Signs"* by Wayne Hancock. It had been a long day. He had been driving for eight hours straight and he was looking forward to some fluffy pillows, a quiet room, and WI-FI Internet access. He liked to stay at the "Hamptons" because he was generally satisfied with most of the hotels in the Hilton chain. He found them to be clean, organized, with good accommodations, .. such as a pool and exercise room. Sanjo liked to stay in shape while he was on the road. And, (he fantasized) …there was always a slim chance that he might bump into some female celebrity while working out. But the best value on the road, he believed, were the Hampton's because they had all of the amenities of the better hotels, … but at a lower price. He liked value. Then again, he also liked the *Courtyard Marriotts*, *Fairfield Inn*, and the *Holiday Inn* chain, as well as the numerous *Holiday Inn Express* hotels that were close to expressways and corresponding exits when he traveled. Though, his final selection would depend on where he was traveling, and the "newness" of each hotel.

He pulled into the hotel parking lot and parked his pick-up truck in a spot close to the front entrance. Then he made his way to the check-in desk. The gal at the front desk was friendly and efficient. She assured him that his Hilton Honors number was recorded, explained the value related to his Gold membership status, handed him a bottled water, and directed him to the elevator for room 329. He was anxious to get to his room and relax, set up his computer, and just chill. He also wanted to "Google" the words *Albert Camus* to get the Wikipedia version of the author's background, and check to see whether he could find the quote that he had tried to remember earlier. Actually, Sanjo believed that *God* was trying to help him get ahead, but that Sanjo had always managed to find a way to screw things up. But he was trying to be better, which is also why he wanted to Google® the subject of "Quantum Jumping" to determine whether it might help his quest for enlightenment.

Sanjo used the "keycard" to unlock the door to room 329, and entered. He dragged his roller bag into the room and shut the door. Then he threw his bag onto one of the double beds and unzipped it, put his toilet kit in the bathroom, and positioned his laptop on the desk. The room was fresh and clean. He was happy. It was 7:08 pm. It had been a long day.

After a quick shower to help relieve the stress and relax his muscles, he reorganized his belongings in his room, then sat down at his laptop and entered the correct code for the wireless network to surf the web, and just unwind. He checked his e-mail, responded to a couple of messages, checked a couple of his favorite blogs, like Yahoo Finance, *Jesse's Café Américain, Zerohedge, The Slog*, and *The Daily Bell*, and browsed a few current events. Another thing that he enjoyed was checking for good deals on e-bay like inexpensive, foreign, early-dated numismatic gold and silver coins that might be available. He believed that the US Federal Reserve was debasing the US Dollar, and he preferred to hedge himself against a future financial crisis. What a great time to be alive he thought, with so much information available via the "web", anyone could "Google" virtually any topic and find answers to perplexing questions, like; *Are vegetarians allowed to eat french toast?* Or, *if we follow generally acceptable vegetarian guidelines, how will this help our current situation when planet Nibiru approaches planet earth?* Of course, one problem with this way of thinking was that "Google" was tracking the "hits" based on individual interest, therefore, there was likely to be a built-in bias when trying to access new information.

Before it became too late, Sanjo decided that he had better call home to touch base with his wife to let her know that he would be traveling a week longer than he had originally planned, … so that she wouldn't worry, and could plan around his schedule. Of course, Marissa was always glad to hear Sanjo's familiar voice; a voice that she had known from the first time she had met him and his sailor buddies at the *California Club*, so many years ago. So, he dialed her number, had a quick chat to let her know that he had made it safely to a hotel in Des Moines, then asked her to call back later if she wanted to talk more. They both wanted to just "chill" after a long day, so they kept the conversation short.

After their exchange, Sanjo returned to his computer, clicked the "Google" link, then typed in the words *Quantum Jumping*. He selected a site at www.quantumjumping.com with the following result;

"Quantum Jumping is a visualization process where you use your mind to **'jump'** into parallel dimensions, and gain creativity, knowledge, wisdom, skills and inspiration from alternate versions of yourself.

This happens through a phenomenon known as "**thought transference**." You see, although the solidity of our world seems indisputable, Quantum Theory suggests that our physical reality is nothing but a very elaborate mirage. A super- hologram of information and energy. A *Matrix*.

According to this theory, the chair you're sitting on, your computer, your house, your car, everything that exists around you, could be an **illusion**.

So then how do we see, touch, feel, and smell the things that surround us if none of it really exists?

The answer is that all physical matter is the result of particles vibrating at a certain frequency. A frequency that if you alter, change or amplify in any way, you change your physical and current reality.

We all know from physics class that if you increase the vibrational frequency of water particles through heat energy, you create steam and if you slow them down by removing heat energy, you create ice. And just like heat, our thoughts too are energy."

The story of how Sanjo and Cassandra reconnected is intriguing, and may help to explain why Sanjo preferred Hilton hotels, over other hotels while traveling. Perhaps that too, was somehow linked to Quantum Mechanics or some new harmonic frequency. The dormant flame between them had been rekindled in the hotel bar at a Hilton hotel in downtown

Minneapolis some years earlier, after they had both left the Philippines under different circumstances.

When Sanjo was discharged from active duty, he took advantage of the GI Bill to go back to school and learn new skills. Jobs were not easy to find in his hometown of Cedar Rapids in the mid-70's when he returned home. Therefore, school was one of the better options available to help prepare him for the future and readjust to civilian life. Like Redhouse, Melnik, Valero, and his other pals before him, he had flown back to California from the Philippines, with orders to be processed and let out. The process took a couple of weeks, so Sanjo decided to spend the extra time with some friends in Martinez who had already been discharged, while he continued to work on his old pickup truck at the Naval base. He very much enjoyed their company during his short stay in California, but it soon became time to say his goodbyes for the journey eastward. One day he would return he said, but he never did. When he arrived back in Iowa he applied to a variety of colleges, and was accepted at a good state college in Des Moines where he decided to pursue a degree in business. Sanjo had a little difficulty adjusting to college life at first, but eventually settled in, and ultimately graduated with a Bachelor's degree in Business Administration. That degree led to a couple of job offers with mid-sized companies in the Des Moines area, one of which he accepted as a buyer in the grain business. As was often the case in those days, about a year after working with the original company, Sanjo was recruited away from the first company and was offered a similar job, with higher pay and better benefits with a competitor company, if he agreed to move north to Minneapolis, Minnesota. Sanjo accepted the higher pay, better benefits, and more active lifestyle, and moved to Minneapolis. As part of the package, the new company paid his moving expenses, and initial living expenses, and put him up at the Hilton Inn in downtown Minneapolis for a month while he looked for an apartment to rent. That all worked out well for Sanjo as he planted his feet in Minnesota for the next few years. In fact, he liked the hotel, and the adjoining bar so well that he would visit it frequently just to check out the nightlife.

Meanwhile, back in the Philippines, Marissa Marikit (aka "Cassandra") had become quite disenchanted with the bar scene, especially after the turmoil in Southeast Asia had ended, and the hustle and bustle within

Olongapo had become sufficiently mundane. Although she had been raised in a small village near San Fernando, and had actually attended a fairly respectable Catholic school, she no longer felt that there were many long-term career opportunities with her present occupation. The other thing that changed her way of thinking, and actually changed her life, was having a child. During their last deployment to the Philippines, Petty Officers Casagrande and Redhouse made their customary trek down to the *California Club* to visit their good friend Cassandra, but she was nowhere to be found. Her friends at the club told them that she had returned to her village for a while to spend some time with her folks, and that she wasn't expected to return to the club. So, although they enjoyed their final visit to Subic Bay, they both missed Cassandra deeply, but also believed that she was gone for good, which may have been best for everyone. The other thing that bothered them both was that the main street was now paved with cement. Olongapo now appeared like many other South Pacific cities to the two sailors, and therefore actually 'felt foreign' to them. They preferred to remember the city the way it had been in their earlier days, when Olongapo was more like the *Wild West*.

In the end, after Marissa's son was born, she returned to the *California Club* to work for a short while to earn some needed cash. But she soon realized that the situation was untenable, and she needed to make some permanent changes, and began to plan accordingly. She needed a new identity. She wasn't getting any younger, her biological clock was ticking, and she now had a son, with no father. Fortunately, she knew a close friend from a nearby village that had moved to Escanaba, Michigan in the USA, and had married an American citizen that worked for the telephone company there. Her friend was quite delighted with America, and had written to Marissa to explain her current situation. When her friend invited Marissa to visit her in northern Michigan, she decided that it must be serendipity. Her friend also said that there was a program available through the US government that would allow her to emigrate to America and work under a visa program. And, if she liked it, they might help support her quest towards finding work and becoming a US citizen within five years. Marissa found the prospect of moving to America exciting after meeting so many gregarious American servicemen. So, after a couple months of careful thought and discussions with her family, she collected a few of her personal belongings and flew to Escanaba via Minneapolis, to experience life in America. She left her young son Francis with her parents in the village for a short time until she could get settled, not knowing what would happen in the following few months. She had picked the name *Francis* to name him after *St. Francis* as well as Frank Valero, whom she believed to be the father of her son. Frank's real name was also Francis Valero, but he preferred to be called 'Frank'. Her ultimate plan was to get her feet on the ground in the United States, then return to the Philippines, retrieve her family, and ultimately improve everyone's life. In fact, her close relatives encouraged the move, and were fully in favor of the arrangement.

Her early days in Escanaba were enjoyable for the most part, and the travel there in the later 70's was a pleasant event. She had even met a sailor on the airplane on the long flight over the Pacific Ocean, which also helped the transition, and made the voyage more enjoyable. They talked about Olongapo and Subic Bay and the various clubs along the strip, as well as their very different personal backgrounds and experiences. They even agreed to write to each other when they arrived at their final destinations, … which they never did. When she arrived in Michigan, the weather in Escanaba that summer seemed rather hot to her. She had always heard how cold it was in the northern states. So, she was a bit surprised, yet delighted with the fact that the climate was similar to her home. However, she was not getting any younger at 26 years of age, so after spending a few months with her friends in the upper peninsula of Michigan, she began to explore other options. She was open to any suggestion that might help her move off of dead center, and there really wasn't much happening in Escanaba anyway for a girl with her background and exceptional experiences. As it happened, her friend told her about another opportunity with the phone company for "office" type work if she was willing to move near Duluth, Minnesota. She had never heard of Escanaba or Duluth while she was growing up in the Philippines, so she was intrigued about the prospect of moving to a larger city located on another one of the Great Lakes. Living on a large northern lake sounded so "woodsy" and serene to Marissa at the time. From her short stay in Escanaba, she learned that there wouldn't be any palm trees growing on Lake Superior, and she had never seen snow in her entire life. Therefore, the thought of living in Minnesota frightened her a bit.

The managers at the Minnesota phone company were constantly promoting "Diversity" in the work place, and were thrilled at the prospect of hiring a young Filipino girl to come to work with them in Duluth. They wanted to learn more about her background and make her feel welcome. They were sure that she would have many new skills to offer the phone company, and perhaps she had other friends that could relocate, and also help to diversify the mostly Nordic gene pool in Duluth. With time, Marissa's move to Minnesota really did work out quite well. The people in Duluth loved her outgoing personality and poise, and welcomed her with open arms. She was a smart young lady, and learned her new assignments quickly. So much so, that she was promoted twice within the first year, and began to look forward to a satisfying career with "Ma Bell". Events transpired so well that she was able to return home for a short period to bring her young son Francis to the States to live with her, and a short time later, her parents moved in with her as well. Subsequently, her promotions led to several training programs, some of which also just happened to be held at the Hilton Inn in downtown Minneapolis several times a year; and the rest of her fate followed.

One evening after work, Sanjo stopped down at the local health club to use the treadmill, lift a few weights, and stretch his wings in downtown Minneapolis. After going through his regular routine for about an hour, he decided to stop over at his favorite watering hole, at the Hilton Inn, to check out the local talent. He liked the Hilton Inn because it was familiar, he felt comfortable with the clientele, and he could unwind before heading back to his two-room apartment. On this particular evening, while sitting at the bar for half an hour, jawboning with the lady bartender, he heard a familiar voice at the end of the bar asking for one of his favorite local beers. Turning to starboard, and looking down past four other guys leaning against the curve in the bar, he glanced over to see Marissa Marikit staring back in his direction. She had just finished a "Ma Bell" training session in one of the hotel conference rooms and had decided to quench her thirst at the hotel bar before heading up to her room. Their eyes transfixed in total tandem, with a wonderful warmth that pierced the stale beer air, and could have easily been a scene from a movie starring Bogart and Bacall; They spent the rest of the night reminiscing about their earlier transgressions in Olongapo before heading up to Marissa's room to rekindle their romance. They began to see more of each other in the days and weeks that followed, as one thing led to another during those many long Minnesota winter months. So Sanjo and "Cassandra" made the transition between their active duty days in the Philippines, the many lonely months during some calmer years, and their life together that ultimately became their new reality. They eventually married, had a daughter of their own, whom they named Anita after Sanjo's mother, and felt delighted in their typical American suburban life residing in a condo at the end of a cul-de-sac.

Now, back in his room at the Hampton Inn, Sanjo was beginning to feel the weight of a very long day. He had driven for many hours, and his mind had traveled far and wide. The comfortable king-sized bed and the fluffy pillows were calling him to throw his head back and enjoy a deep slumber. The television was on, but it could not compete with his tired mind as he propped his head against the backboard of the bed. He would call Richard Redhouse in the morning to see whether they could meet and reminisce. There would be time for everything. And with that, he closed his eyes.

Sanjo awoke abruptly at 2:17 AM to use the head, and then returned to his bed. He turned off the TV that had concluded most of the night's regular programming. He wrote down a couple of notes to himself, then slipped back between the crumpled sheets, and slept until half past 8:00 AM the next morning.

It's What's For Dinner, Indonesia, 1974

43

THE ROAD TO KANSAS

*"Lose an hour, gain an hour. This is your life, and it's
ending one minute at a time. ...*

*If you wake up at a different time, in a different place,
could you wake up as a different person?" Narrator
— Fight Club*

Sanjo awoke to a sunny day and a grumpy stomach. He showered and
shaved, flossed between his teeth, dried between his toes, got dressed, then
took the elevator to the lobby to enjoy a quick breakfast of oatmeal, juice,
English muffin, and fruit. He poured a black cup of coffee from the "free"
pot in the lobby, and returned to his room to check his e-mail. He had
written a note to himself to look up Richard Redhouse's phone number
to call, but actually, he didn't need the note. He found the number in his
address book on his computer and dialed the number. Richard's voicemail
instructed him to leave a short message, so that's what he did. He then
prepared to check out of the hotel, and head toward Kansas. They would
talk later.

Sanjo's early life was not without tribulation. He had fond memories
of growing up in a mobile home park near Albuquerque, New Mexico
until about age ten. However, being the only son of a single mother who
worked as a stripper at a local bar during the day, and a waitress at a
diner at night, he often felt like one of the many tumbleweeds that blew
through the dusty streets of that high-plains Southwest city. His mother,
whose original name was Anita Kelly, had a number of male friends
during Sanjo's younger years in Albuquerque until she met Hank, and later
moved to Iowa. Those early memories were enough to leave Sanjo feeling

vulnerable and guarded in his relationships with others; but the fact that he also attended several religious schools beyond kindergarten, also added to his ponderous perspective of humanity. There were a couple of short stints at some public schools during transitions in a few nameless towns, but for the most part, Sanjo was educated by various nuns, brothers, and monks in scattered towns in the Southwest. Those experiences actually helped Sanjo to form an open mind about people and circumstances, and to avoid unpleasant situations that were often beyond his control. Other than that, he didn't learn much in school, which helped him to avoid being trapped by the philosophies of others, as he developed a mind of his own. His opinion of teachers was essentially that they were good at repeating the same endless bullshit until they actually believed it themselves; when in fact, much of what they taught was unproven. But, Sanjo tried to keep an open mind as he fit the pieces of life's many puzzles together. Life was like a business he decided, and one needed to make proper investments to profit from the experiences. He had a mind for business.

Kansas seemed almost like coming home to him. He had not been to Kansas City in many years, maybe 15 years, and he couldn't remember whether he had ever been to Topeka. He remembered Kansas City as a clean city on the Kansas side, and not so clean on the Missouri side of the river. He remembered some good steak joints and jazz bands somewhere on the street corners in Kansas City, Kansas. And as he drove, feeling the vibrations of the road float through the floorboard to his feet, he listened to country-western tunes on the radio, and sang *"there's some crazy little women there, and I'm gonna get me one ...."* He slapped a disk into the CD player as he drove toward Kansas, listening to a Bob Dylan tune *"It's a Hard Rain's A'Goona Fall"*, as it began to drizzle again.

Richard Redhouse had an altogether different childhood than Sanjo Casagrande. As the eldest boy in a family of five children, growing up in a middle-class residential neighborhood in Rockford, Minnesota, his life was much like many Americans of his era. He was on a local little league baseball team called the "Cardinals" when he was in grade school. In high school, he played football, ran track, was in the school Honor Society while getting decent grades, and was a member of the chess club. His father, Randahl Redhouse, had a responsible job with the local electric co-op company, thereby pulling down a good salary, while his mother stayed at home to raise the children. So, his childhood days were quite typical, and average, growing up in the 50's and 60's. The family could afford good schooling and medical benefits, nice clothes for their kids (the boys all wore Gant shirts in their teens), and they were active in their local church and community. This culture also made him an attractive candidate for CIA recruitment. And, what average kid doesn't want to be a future James Bond character? So, with his inquisitive mind, and lust for adventure, Dick Redhouse followed a perfunctory path.

Growing up in a small town did have some drawbacks though. Throughout his life he would often ponder, and try to better understand the way the real world worked. Partly because of the way that he was raised in a small Minnesota town, one child among many, a few awkward friends, and little access to the larger population, no one advised him regarding some of less obvious lessons in life. He learned many hard lessons by grinding away on his own, through personal experience. Things like, if you don't dry between your toes after you shower, you get athlete's feet, and it hurts. Lesson; Dry between your toes after you shower. Other things, that may have been apparent to others, but were less obvious to Redhouse, were things that he learned in boot camp after he joined the Navy. The Navy taught him how to fold his clothes correctly, how to properly make his bed, how to march in step with others, how to follow orders (which he never quite mastered), how to use a shirt or a pair of pants as a flotation device, how to float *without* a flotation device, and how to floss. They were also taught, "If it moves, salute it! If it doesn't, paint it!" Prior to these events he went through life with bad breath, messy clothes, an aversion to authority figures, and a general fear of water. And, he never liked to paint. The Navy changed some of that. With this new knowledge he began to build more confidence. And, as he learned new things, he began to hunger for ways to improve his life.

Armed with a thirst for knowledge, Redhouse used the GI Bill to return to college after being discharged and continued his quest for life, liberty, and happiness. Still, success eluded him. So it was with some effort, that he began to ponder one of the more perplexing problems in his life. And as he questioned things, he began to understand what made the world work. What constitutes fame, fortune, and power. Why some people are at ease with themselves and display great confidence, while others squander life's many opportunities. It was all about having "skin in the game". It was so obvious. Why hadn't he seen it before?

He finally understood that without a share in the process, one is lost. People with a hand in the action benefit, while those without a stake lose. It's what Adam Smith, Benjamin Franklin, Thomas Jefferson, Henry Ford, Ayn Rand, and others knew, he decided. It's why Capitalism works, yet centralized government is left wanting. It's why entrepreneurs strive to own a business, while governments confiscate wealth and reallocate it. It's why some people live well, and others don't. It's the dirty little secret that, if you can't figure it out for yourself, no one is going to tell you. Redhouse was also once told that he had an amazing grasp of the obvious. It wasn't meant as a compliment, but Redhouse took it as one. He believed in limited government; that people should "carry their own water", and that the definition of compassion was "helping people to help themselves". Still, that didn't mean that people should "help themselves" to other people's property. In his time, he knew all too well that governments were sequestering a large share of peoples' wealth. Yet virtually a third of the population was content with accepting government handouts like unemployment, disability, food stamps, social security, and other subsidies. So, Redhouse began to ask the question "how can I control a share in the process and make money while I sleep, without getting handouts from the government?" This was something that he and Sanjo had in common, and had discussed on occasion over countless pints of ale. Added to that, there were more ponderous questions that perplexed the two gentlemen, and begged more definitive answers including; What is money; what is value, and what is wealth? In this electronic age where thousands, millions, billions, and even trillions of dollars could be transferred globally in milliseconds through SWIFT accounts, which merely amounted to a mountain of digits, how could he get a share? What good is money if you can't collect it and enjoy it? He asked himself rhetorically.

Redhouse felt that he had been going to school for a long time, but hadn't really learned much useful 'real world' information. Consequently, he decided that the best way for him to get a share in the process, from a constructive point of view, or as he liked to say "from a pipeline perspective", was to pretend that he was a filter; insert himself into the pipeline, and collect a portion of the money stream as it traveled through the pipe. This was also a 'pipefitter's perspective' he decided. He believed that the best way to implement his plan was to become an "agent" or "broker", collecting his small share of the profits from the world's large pool of wealth. Now, he just had to figure out which fetid pool to exploit.

As Redhouse began to distill many of the more complex issues in his head, he would often attempt to synthesize his thoughts by writing them down. This gathering of words often resulted in rhyme, as if the input was being transmitted from an outside source. The result was often a reminder in the form of a poem. And so he wrote;

School Call

I've been going to school a long time now,
It seems a sort of bind;
The school is called the school of life,
I've been taking one course at a time.

I started walking at sixteen months
They told me I was slow.
But I just do things my own way
The only way I know.

Once I knew a gambler,
His sleeves held many tricks.
But now his sleeves are empty,
And he's into politics.

If you haven't a million by twenty-five,
I'm told you never will.
Unless, of course, you pay your way
By dipping in the till.

I asked one man what I must do
To put me in the pink?
He told me in one simple word
That I should stop and THINK.

I once had many questions
'cause I used to think a lot.
But now I've heard the answers;
That's why I drink a lot.

I'm getting lost for answers
As to just what I must do,
To get ahead in this backward world
Before I bid adieu.

So, I'll just keep taking courses
'til I find something I like;
or, wind up empty minded
like the rest of mankind's psych.

But what have I to lose at all?
Indeed! What have I to gain?
Just another school call!
To me, it's all the same!

Jaak - South China Seas, 1973

USS Flint (AE-32), Underway Replenishment
with the USS Kitty Hawk (CVA-63)

Gunner's Mates. South China Sea, USS Flint (AE-32), 1974

Upon checking out of the Hampton, the girl behind the counter handed Sanjo a receipt with a zero balance. Sanjo checked the rate and noted the additional taxes for State Occupancy Tax of 12%, City Tax of 5%, and the parking fee. Then he walked to his truck, loaded his luggage, backed out of his parking space, and turned the truck toward Kansas. He would try Dick Redhouse's phone number again while on the road.

What Sanjo didn't know was that several years earlier, Dick had changed his name to "Jack". He had never liked the name "Dick", so after he left the service he went to see a lawyer and had his name legally changed to *Jack Redhouse*. Jack sounded a lot like Dick, he decided, but without the reference to his male anatomy. He didn't think that a man should be called "Dick", any more than a woman should be called by a part of her anatomy. It was crass. So he had it changed. At first, he asked that people just call him "RJ" since his middle name was John. And, for a time, he even signed his name as *R. John Redhouse*, but it took too much time to write. Then he switched to just *R. J. Redhouse*. That lasted for about a year. But "RJ" sounded too aristocratic to him, and he preferred the free-and-easy sound of "Jack". Therefore, when Sanjo finally did reach him on the phone, calling him from another rest area during a short break from the road, the reply on the other end of the line was; "No, this is *Jack* Redhouse", and he went through the long explanation of how he had legally changed his name; and Sanjo, knowing his history, understood 'Jacks' trepidation.

"So, 'Jack', how have you been?", asked Sanjo. "It's been a few years since we were 'steaming' in the party ports of the Pacific! It may be time to catch up with a couple of pints, and compare notes" And they caught up and reminisced about a few of their past exploits in the back-alley bars, and hapless whore houses, in the salty seaside ports of the South China Sea that, after a while, like the girls throughout Southeast Asia, all began to look alike. Jack reminded Sanjo of the time that he had crawled out through an iron-barred window onto a ledge five stories above the street in Bangkok, after a drinking binge, and his shipmates called him "Spiderman" for a couple of months until the novelty wore off. "Yeah! It's lucky we survived those years" he said. Then, Sanjo reminded Jack about the time that Billy Blahnik pulled down his trousers in a bar after betting a Marine that he had his name tattooed on his ass, and they both had a good laugh. "Yes, those were fun times", said Jack. "A lot has changed since then."

"Yes they have, for the better", said Sanjo.

Then Jack continued, "But, the times that I miss the most are the many nights that we spent at the bars along the strip in Olongapo, like the *California Club*, and the different Filipino girls that hung out there."

"I often wonder what Cassandra is doing after all these years?", he said inquisitively.

"Hahaha, it's funny that you bring that up Dick (forgetting that his name was now Jack), "Cassandra and I were married over fifteen years ago" said Sanjo. And the phone went silent for a bit.

"Excuse me? Came the question after a long pause.

"Yeah, it's funny how things work out" said Sanjo, "Marissa came to the states a few years after we got out, and we ran into each other in a bar in Minneapolis,

... and, well, one thing led to another. We tied the knot a few years after she came to the States. She's now a U.S. citizen" Sanjo said matter-of-factly. "She sometimes asks what ever happened to you?", he taunted. "Who's Marissa? Asked Jack.

"Oh, .. *Marissa Marikit* is *Cassandra's* real name" said Sanjo. "The word *Marikit* means 'Beauty' in Tagalog" Sanjo said knowingly. "I didn't know that!" said Jack.

"Which reminds me, that's one of the reasons that I'm calling. I'm headed down your way, and I thought you might like to get together for a beer, and catch up on old times. Are you up for that?

"You're in Kansas?" asked Jack.

"Well I'm getting close". Said Sanjo. "I spent last night in Des Moines, and I'm headed down your way now. I have some extra time on my hands because of a glitch in my schedule, so rather than drive all the way back to Duluth, I decided to drive down your way" he continued.

"That's interesting!" Jack responded incredulously. "Sure, ... I'd love to get together. Give me a call when you get near Topeka, and I'll meet you for a couple of beers at one of my favorite watering holes!"

After the call ended, Sanjo called Marissa at work to let her know that he was heading down to Kansas to meet with Dick Redhouse. He hadn't discussed the issue in his call to her the night before since they were both tired, and at the time, he didn't know whether he would actually be able to hook up with Redhouse. He also told her that Dick had changed his name to Jack, so that now he was actually going down to meet with 'Jack' Redhouse. Marissa was surprised but understanding, knowing what pals they had been in the past. "Maybe you should change your name to Sanjay" she said mocking him. "I don't think I'd make a very good Sanjay" he replied. "It's hard enough for me to remember to call Dick, … Jack".

THE JACK OF CLUBS

*"In this reality, an infinite amount of universes exist, and
in them, there are infinite versions of you waiting to be
discovered. Anything that can be, already is".* - http://
www.quantumjumping.com/about/about-qj

By the summer of 1982, Richard Redhouse (or, let's just call him
"Jack" for the sake of simplicity), was well into a firm career path. He had
established some credibility after graduating from engineering school,
and was beginning to build a solid foundation for a bright future. His
years in the Navy, working as a marine mechanic, with his prior years in
construction, had all provided Jack with qualifications required by large
international construction firms that held major contracts on expansive
projects in the middle east, and which also had strong ties to US and
foreign military agencies around the world.

Upon graduation, he was hired by a well-known and prominent
construction firm to work on a wastewater treatment project close to home
that ultimately led to many similar projects in more distant places. He
longed to return to Southeast Asia, and he dreamed of one day returning
to the Philippines to see his young girlfriend Cassandra; but alas, that
never transpired. Instead, Jack began to achieve more responsibility and a
favorable reputation as he moved to new projects in far off foreign lands.
Back in Minnesota, his family and neighborhood friends would hear about
his exploits and get his occasional postcard that would serve to make him
into somewhat of a legendary figure back at his hometown high school,
where he was already held in high regard. There were several rumors
circulating that Jack had joined the CIA, and that the construction work
was just a front for covert activities for the US military. Of course, Jack

fed these rumors whenever he returned to Rockford, Minnesota, so many of his friends and relatives just accepted the fact that Jack was in the CIA. Eventually, he wound up in the Middle East working on secure military projects that provided him with a very good income, plenty of travel to exotic places, and a circle of friends that networked to keep themselves in the loop of that lucrative lactation. The pay was good to begin with, but the fact that he could also keep most of what he earned due to a tax-free income status while working overseas, along with per diem payments for his living expenses, allowed Jack to accumulate a sizeable next egg for the future, and eventual retirement. Because he lived abroad, and occasionally entered into a long distance romance, his life was filled with several lost opportunities for meeting a permanent soul mate. He tried on-line dating a few times, but that also ended in disappointment. Eventually, he accepted this fate as "a price to pay" for his liberal life, and enjoyed the freedom and lack of commitment that came with his less conventional lifestyle. That was his conundrum. He had never married, had suffered many lost relationships, sometimes as a result of political, religious, philosophical, or just plain stubborn personal beliefs, but eventually came to relish his life as a sovereign individual.

After the Navy, Redhouse tried to stay in touch with Sanjo Casagrande and Frank Valero, two of his old steaming buddies, as they all made their transitions from military to civilian life. In the early days, they had all tried to look each other up back in California at their home ports, after each of their WESPAC cruises ended. The bond between them was strong and they kept in contact with one another in those early years. But, with time, they drifted apart as they dallied in different directions. Somewhere in the interim, after his move to Kansas, and after being jilted once again by one of his nefarious flings, he decided to take up flying to focus on something that might challenge him, lessen his troubles, and provide some enjoyment.

At the time, he had visions of becoming a crop duster. It might be profitable as well as fun, he thought. So, through an acquaintance, he began taking flying lessons in an old Cessna 170 tail dragger. It was owned by a local pilot and flight instructor, and kept at *Forbes Field* in Topeka, Kansas. He discovered that he loved to fly, as it helped him to view his world in a different light. He enjoyed the freedom and sense of adventure that it provided, and it was a great way to escape the mundane reality of everyday life in Topeka. After a couple of months he soloed, then went on to get his private pilot's license after about a year of part time instruction, and continued his hobby to the present day. Eventually, many years later, he bought the little blue and white Cessna that he had soloed in years earlier, after the original owner, now a friend, decided to upgrade to a larger plane. It was kept in the same hangar on *Forbes Field* where it had been maintained for many years.

It had been many years since Jack and Sanjo had actually spoken to each other, and so very much had transpired during the in-between years. Also, it was certainly news to Jack that Sanjo had married Cassandra. Jack had mixed feelings about that. Now, Sanjo was on his way to Topeka, so his curiosity was piqued.

After Sanjo finished his call to his wife Marissa, he continued down I-35 through the rolling Missouri farmland towards Kansas City and Topeka. It was much like he had remembered it years earlier. The car and truck traffic began to increase as he approached Kansas City on the Missouri side, with a few new large office complexes cropping up from the middle of the sprawling fields. Residential areas also began to appear as he passed a roadside sign that read EXIT 17 and Liberty KCI Airport ½ MILE. He continued heading South down I- 35 through Pleasant Valley, Claycomo, and Antioch Acres, crossing over the big Missouri River, through downtown Kansas City, Missouri. He picked up the I- 670/I-70 loop and headed west through Kansas City, Kansas, and again marveled at the difference between the Missouri side, and the Kansas side, as he drove. Two completely different cities with the same name, he thought, as he remembered that he needed to call Jack to let him know that he would be in Topeka soon. As he ascended out of the valley through the rolling farmland on the Kansas side heading West, with the twin cities vanishing in his rearview mirror, and the terrain beginning to match the farmland on the Missouri side, he dialed up his cell phone to call Jack back.

"Jack, it's me Sanjo" he said, after reaching Jack on his cell phone. "I just passed through Kansas City, and I'm about 30 miles out. Where would you like to meet?"

"Hi Sanjo, that was quick. Let's meet for lunch at a little place in Topeka called the *Jack of Clubs*" replied Jack. "It's got some great burgers and steaks, as well as some local brews. I've got a few errands to run, but

I can meet you there for lunch, and we can make plans from there. How does that sound?

"Sure", replied Sanjo. "Where is it?"

"When you're coming into Topeka on I-70, you take the I-470 loop south until you reach the state road, 75. Take 75 south to 53rd street. The bar will be on your left" Jack continued. "There's a small airport behind the bar where I keep my plane" said Jack.

"That's interesting. OK, the *Jack of Clubs*. That shouldn't be too difficult. I'll call you if I get lost" said Sanjo. "It's about eleven o'clock now so I'll see you around noon."

"That sounds good Sanjo. I'm looking forward to it", said Jack. "OK. See you soon" Sanjo repeated.

Sanjo continued down I-70 and followed Jack's directions to the state road 75 turnoff, as instructed. He turned south to 53rd street where he spotted the *Jack of Clubs* after traveling a few miles down the road, on the left side of the street, just as Jack had mentioned. He could see a small airport beyond the property where the restaurant sat, and he knew that this must be the correct place. He was a bit surprised by the appearance though. It appeared to Sanjo, having been raised in Albuquerque by his affable mother, that the establishment looked more like a strip club than a restaurant. He looked at his watch and noticed that it was only 11:40 AM, so he decided to do a little reconnaissance before heading into the place. He continued south past the Forbes Field airport entrance with rows of several large grain elevators to his right, until he came to the end of the field and Academy Blvd. He then made a U-turn and headed back north. As he passed the airport entrance the second time, he turned right and drove on to the airport grounds and through the streets leading to the terminal. The airport grounds were impressive with many worn and vacant barracks, as well as an old church with a steeple. A large white water tower read FORBES FIELD across its bulbous tank. As it happens, the airport was on the former site of the Topeka Army Airfield, later known as Topeka Army Air Base. Sanjo made a couple of loops around the grounds, then exited the airport and continued north to the restaurant, parked his truck, and walked inside the *Jack of Clubs*.

What he found looked familiar, and quite similar to places he had visited in the past. He should have known that 'Jack' Redhouse would pick a place like this to have lunch. And, it now made sense that the location was close to an airport. As his eyes adjusted to the dark surroundings, he saw several scantily dressed young ladies waiting on tables bringing food and beverages to an enthused and gratified, mostly male, clientele. He felt grounded. He walked to the back of the bar and found a table in an area that was elevated from the main floor and surrounded by brass rails. There was a row of bench seats along the back wall behind the table where he sat with his back to the wall. He had a good view of the bar and the main floor from where he was perched. A girl danced in the corner.

After a few minutes, a pretty young gal named *Pernicious* approached him, and he suddenly felt like a kid in a candy shop. She had long silky legs attached to high heels, a slender figure under a short skirt, eyes like an Egyptian, and lips that were made to melt in your mind, not in your mouth. Her shag cut hair framed her oval face in a way that made her appear like an avatar. As she bent toward him, her bottomless breasts betrayed her bitty bra, and burst upon him to lend more allure in the limited light. After a long drive, she was a sight for sore eyes.

"Howdy, pardner. My name is *Pernicious*, and I'll be your server" she said. "Welcome to the *Jack of Clubs*! The classiest club in Kansas! Can I bring you a beverage to start?"

"Is that your real name?" asked Sanjo, knowing that it wasn't.

"Of course it is!" she replied, hinting a smile. "Pernicious Mulhaney. My Father named me *Pernicious* because I was born unexpectedly to a family that already had three girls." she said with a voice that sounded a bit like *Holly Hunter*, the movie actress.

"How quaint!" he replied, as he began to feel awkward and a bit old, and even more constrained in the corner.

"Do you have any local draft beers? When in Kansas, do as the Keynesians do" he said, trying to make a joke.

"Sure, consumption helps the economy" *Pernicious* replied, showing that she understood his humor. "We feature a couple of local beers that you might like. We have a *Holy Grail Pale Ale* that has a light copper color, as well as a *Blind Tiger*, that has a darker copper color. Would you like to try one of them? She asked.

"Well, since I'm flying blind here, I'll try the *Blind Tiger*" he replied with a wink, preferring the name of the beer, more than the dark copper color, but enjoying their exchange. Then he felt a little stupid.

"Good choice, I'll bring it right over, sir", she said, which made him feel older yet. As she returned to the bar, he decided that she walked like an Egyptian too.

When Jack entered the bar, Sanjo hardly recognized him. For one thing, the light level was low, and there were several attractive girls walking back and forth distracting his gaze. But as Jack ambled closer, a halogen beam of light froze his familiar frame, and Sanjo recognized his gait. He looked like the same old 'Jack', but with a bit more gravity on his leading edge then Sanjo had remembered. Still, he looked like the same sailor buddy from the good ol' days. His square jaw sported a short gray beard, and he hadn't lost much hair on top of his head. He wore a cotton jacket over a checkered shirt, with faded blue jeans and cowboy boots that shouted, 'I'm from Kansas', and made him appear like he was away from the ranch chores just long enough to grab a sandwich.

"Hey, Sanjo! Good to see ya", Jack said as he spotted him in the back corner where he expected to find him. He pulled up a chair next to his old pal just as *Pernicious* came up from behind.

"One *Blind Tiger*" she said as she removed the beer from her tray and placed it on the table in front of Sanjo. She reached around with the same cold hand to Jack and said "Hi, I'm Pernicious!"

"How delicious!" said Jack, warming her hand as their eyes met. "What can I get 'cha, darlin'" she asked.

"I'm searching for the Holy Grail" said Jack, and Sanjo understood that he had used that line before. Same old Jack, he thought.

"Comin' right up tiger" she replied, and then Sanjo knew that Jack was a regular.

Pernicious then turned away as they both watched her sweet retreat.

"Well this is a welcome surprise! Good to see you Sanjo" Jack repeated. "How's life treatin' ya, ..and what brings you to my backyard?"

"Life's a battle Jack, but I'm doin' OK." said Sanjo, trying to pick up on the lingo.

"Yes, life's a battle. But, are ya winning?" asked Jack.

"I win some, lose some, and some are rained out!" said Sanjo, trying to go with the flow. "On this particular trip, the game was rained out, and that's why I'm here. As I mentioned earlier, my business meeting in Des Moines was cancelled, so I decided to stretch my road trip to visit my old friend 'Dick' Redhouse, and maybe learn a few things along the way" he said. "Actually, the meeting wasn't cancelled as much as it was postponed. It was pushed back a week. So, I'm just fillin' in some dead space until I head back north to complete the mission. I thought of you and your poems and decided that it might be time to look you up. As you used to say *'Nothing is real, it's just what you make it'*! So, I'm making it real. Are you still a philosopher?"

"Ha-ha" Jack chuckled. "Well, I haven't written many poems lately, if that's what you mean Sanjo. On the ship I wrote poems to relieve the boredom. It was either that, or play another game of *Spades*; but actually, I did some of both" he said. "No, lately I've been busy with the ranch, and trying to do some of the things I was putting off, even though the world seems to be spinning out of control as we speak" Jack continued. "As you say, pursuing a new reality. New vibrations. Everything changes, and I'm just changing with it" he said. "According to some, we are entering a new dimension where vibrations of the earth and within our inner selves are increasing in frequency and amplitude. The earth is actually a huge electromagnet with it's own gravitational pull, interfacing with other planets in the universe, and altering magnetic fields as it spins through infinite space. Some people say that we are all integrally connected with each other and with the planets. The ancients knew this, and with all of our technology we are just learning this again; but it has all been known for a long, long time. Whereas, the earth's atmosphere resonates at a relatively low frequency of about 7.83 Hertz, some people believe that frequencies will begin to increase to 11 or 12 Hertz as we enter a new age; A fifth turning. This may bring more harmony to our world as we experience new levels of communication like mental telepathy, and enlightened levels of emotion."

"You don't say," said Sanjo, sipping some of his *Blind Tiger*. Jack continued, "Everyone lives within their own sense of reality and what they perceive to be real events. What's real to one person may seem unreal to another, and therefore there's a breakdown in communication between people in general. It's consciousness! We all need to get on the same wavelength. Einstein knew it, Max Planck knew it, even Aristotle understood it; and, if you amplify the frequency, the structure of the matter will change."

"All of physical matter, everything we have around us, is the result of a frequency. And what that also means is, if you amplify the frequency the structure of the matter will change." http://youtu.be/y9bVd3BspIQ

"So, you are still a philosopher," said Sanjo. "Have you seen any spaceships lately?"

"Haa-ha. Perhaps. If that's what you want to call it Sanjo. Actually, my thinking hasn't changed much since I wrote that poem years ago. I've just expanded my views on the subject as I learn new information. And, I'm not really sure that they're my views. I may just be channeling Max Planck. I don't know. These things just come into my head, and I write them down or repeat them. Does that make me a philosopher, or just someone else's Muppet? Have you ever noticed as you travel around the world that people everywhere often seem to be in tune with one another? And, you can generally tell quickly if a person is good or bad, or whether you can communicate with them on some ethereal level, wherever you go? Or how about the way that people communicate with their dog or cat or pet bird; or for that matter with porpoises and whales; or people's relationships with plants? Do you remember when we were in different ports around the world, going from town to town, and bar to bar, that we could read people quickly, and react accordingly? Do you remember how the girls in Olongapo often seemed to know whether we had been with another girl in another bar, or whether they knew if we had honorable intentions? Have you ever noticed how married couples seem to know when their partners have cheated on them, or how they communicate without saying a word? Have you ever connected with someone immediately on a personal level as if they knew what you were thinking without saying a word? Have you ever been in love with someone that understood how you felt, and knew what you were thinking, without telling them how you feel? Do you know what love is? And how about that *Pernicious*? Isn't she something? Somewhat of an Egyptian don't you think? It's a level of intelligence, and it's increasing. I call it the 'KNOW'. Some people just have an innate intelligence. You have the KNOW Sanjo. And you know that you have the KNOW. That's one of the reasons that you're here now."

"Wow! You're beginning to scare me Jack!"

"Ha-ha. There you go again Sanjo. But you 'know' what I'm talking about don't you? You may say I'm a philosopher, … but you should have been a priest, Sanjo!"

"Then again, priests don't usually marry. Speaking of marriage, and people in the know, how's Cassandra?"

"Well, Marissa's just fine, Jack. I called her and told her that I was heading down to see you and she said to say 'Hello'" She always had a 'thing' for you. But I guess you knew that."

"Yeah. She was one of my favorite people. Again, that just shows to go ya, we're all connected in a funny kind of way."

"OK, I think I get it; I'm you, and you're me, and we're all one big happy family" Sanjo said with a grin.

"I don't know Sanjo. I really don't have all the answers. I'm simply trying to understand the big picture like everyone else. I'm just sayin', we have a lot in common, and even if we think we KNOW, there's more that we don't know, than we do know at this point. I'm just tryin' to figure it out like everyone else. But, I think changes are coming."

"That's confusing, and perhaps a bit of a contradiction.," said Sanjo.

But Jack continued, "With the Internet, there's a lot of info at our fingertips; almost too much really. But it sure is a great resource; and with everything moving so fast I'm just tryin' to put the puzzle together. We didn't have that luxury when we were floatin' around the South China Sea. Hell, they hadn't invented the PC, let alone the Internet back in the '70's. And a good electric typewriter was considered high tech."

"Fair enough" said Sanjo, trying to change the topic. "But, I will say for a fact, that this *Blind Tiger* really hits the spot after a long drive."

"Yes, and as I said, I'm still searching for the Holy Grail" replied Jack, getting back on track.

"So, when will it all end Jack?" "When will what end Sanjo?" "Well, in your poem you wrote;

Nothing is real,

It's just what we make it. We're making the motions, While we really just fake it. They feed us the data, and like fools we take it' Trying to expand our mind; Instead we just bake it.

When will it end,

This follow the leader?

"Ha-ha. That's right! Good memory Sanjo! So, maybe it will all end when we don't have to follow a leader, in a new dimensional age, when we're all thinking on the same wave pattern, and can agree on all subjects" replied Jack. "I don't know. I just made that up. I was 23 years old. That's a while back. I've slept a lot of nights since then."

"Some things never change", said Sanjo.

Pernicious returned with a *Holy Grail Pale Ale* and placed it on the table in front of Jack.

"Here you go Tiger" she said. "Can I get you guys something to eat?" Jack looked at her warmly and said "Thanks, Carol. How about a couple of good *Hungry Jack* burgers with the works". Carol just smiled and turned away to let them talk.

"Carol?" asked Sanjo.

"Yeah. That's her real name. Carol Mulhaney. She's one of the owners of the *Jack of Clubs*".

"Wow. Nothing is real! What else don't I know?"

"Well, I've known Carol for a few years. I met her shortly after I moved to Topeka. We dated awhile, then one day she told me that she wanted to start her own business, and asked me whether I would like to invest in a new enterprise. After thinking it over, I decided that it might be a good idea to have a place like this near the airport where the local customers could get a burger and a beer, and enjoy some diversion from the real world. We put a business plan together, went to the local bank, bought this building cheap on a commercial foreclosure deal, and the rest is history. The *Jack of Clubs* was born. We've been operating for about three years at a nice profit."

"Jeez, Jack, she's young enough to be your daughter! Robbing the cradle, are we?"

"Well, yes, she's young, maybe it was the chemistry."

"Really, Jack! .. anything else that you're holding back?" asked Sanjo. "Well, yeah. Frank Valero is also one of the partners in the business."

"I think I need another beer", said Sanjo, surprised. "How does Frank fit in?"

"So, when we were setting things up, I needed a little more capital to put the deal together" he said. "I called Frank, since I knew that he had socked away a little cash working at the shipyards down south, and I asked him whether he would like to invest in a little sideline business. He was interested, so he put up some money for a share of the profit. It's worked out pretty well for him", answered Jack.

"So, what's the rest of the story Jack? What else have you been doing for the past twenty years?"

"Well, that might take a while Sanjo".

"I made a lot of money working in the Middle East. I don't need to go into the details. Quite a few projects, working tax free as an ex-pat, and I socked most of it away in bonds, equities that paid good dividends, and other profitable investments. No family, no bills, just a lot of cash over the years with no taxes. I bought a little 200-acre ranch outside of town, with a few head of cattle and some crops, and I've been working it. Life is good. But I don't know if it's going to last. The world is going to shit, and like everyone else, I'm just trying to compensate. It costs a lot of money to run a ranch. I hedge my bets on the commodity exchanges, and the bankers just steal my money, then laugh about it, and pay themselves big bonuses. Now the Fed is bailing out the big banks with taxpayer money and devaluing the US dollar, so my money is worth less. Meanwhile, I shoulder all the risk for my operation, with no help from anyone. The banks won't lend, and it's a race to the bottom with every other Western nation doing the same thing. What's the answer? Everyone's in it for themselves and taking all they can get until the system crashes. Where's the rationale in that? Maybe I'm better off selling out and buying a spread in Chile or Colombia; getting a little hacienda with a great big gate, and dining with the local chiquitas" said Jack. "We've only got a few good years left after all. And as Keynes famously said, ... in the end we're all dead."

"That's a rather fatalistic view of the future" said Sanjo emphatically.

"Well, yes. It could go the other way, but only if there's some kind of outside divine intervention, I believe. On that subject, do you think it's possible to read someone's mind Sanjo?"

"Maybe some people can do it. I've never been very good at it!" said Sanjo. "Well, how do new ideas come to a person's mind? Is it really just that necessity is the mother of invention"? "I'm sure that there's some of that. And, without a need, there's probably no demand, so good ideas get dropped. However, there are an awful lot of good ideas out there just floating around in space if we have the desire to grab them and implement them. And, of course, there needs to be some payback with it. I've often been afraid to think about a new idea too much for fear that, if I think about it too much, someone else will think about it too, and just take my idea. After all, we're all connected, so the thoughts are all out there. How did Einstein get all of his bright ideas? He flunked Algebra for Christ's sake."

"Don't swear Jack"

"Somehow, his inspiration was from an outside source. He may have just been selected as an appropriate venue to translate ideas about light and relativity to the outside world. Perhaps his mind just worked at a different frequency that allowed ideas to be received more readily. Of course, he probably had the determination to pursue those ideas to a point where he had more clarity. Or, maybe it was for fame or fortune, or love. But something inspired him, and something drove him to follow through. Or, how about Thomas Edison, or Benjamin Franklin, or Thomas Jefferson? What drove them to pursue so many of their great ideas?"

"How do you sleep at night Jack?" insisted Sanjo. "By the way, how did you come up with the name *Jack of Clubs*?" he asked.

"That's a good question Sanjo. Actually, if you think about it, if you look at a typical *Jack of Clubs* playing card, you'll see the same two figures inverted, as if they are the same person operating in a different plane or dimension. It's almost as if one Jack is an alias of the other. It begs the question, 'Who do you want to be?' And, since my name is 'Jack', and this is a 'club', *Jack of Clubs* seemed like a natural. Sort of like you said earlier; 'I am you, you are me, and we're all one big happy family'. We're all connected Sanjo, and seeking our identity. The *Jack of Clubs* simply reminds me that we can be whomever we want to be, … and the name just seemed to fit."

"OK, that sounds like a lot of bullshit, but I think I get it!" said Sanjo, as he began to feel the effects of the second *Blind Tiger*. "So now I'm Jack, and you're Sanjo" said Sanjo. "How do you like my club?" "Do you have a place to stay this evening? Would you like to stay at the ranch?"

"Haha. Sure, Jack" said Jack. "I think I'd like that. But let's eat lunch first; then we'll take a quick ride out to the ranch."

Sanjo: "Jack, you hardly touched your beer. Are you not fond of the *Holy Grail*?"

Jack: "Quite rightly, Sanjo. But normally, I like to keep twenty-four hours between the bottle and the throttle" he said. "And, when we get to the ranch, I have two cases of *Holy Grail Pale Ale* that I keep cold in the barn".

With that, they devoured their *Hungry Jack* burgers with a side of fries that *Pernicious* had carefully snuck between them as they were hashing out the world's problems. When they had finished, Jack and Sanjo walked over to the bar, said their "See ya' laters" to *Pernicious*, walked outside to Sanjo's truck, hopped in, and drove to the hanger on *Forbes Field* where Jack kept his Cessna 170.

DOWN ON THE FARM

"Give me a place to stand on, and I will move the Earth."
— Archimedes 287-212 BC.

On the way to the hangar they continued their conversation. Jack told Sanjo more about the plane and the ranch, as they discussed plans for the afternoon. The plane was kept on the south side of the airport in an old Quonset hut that was left over from World War II. Sanjo headed south, back down Topeka Boulevard until he came to Academy, turned left, and listened, as Jack filled in a few of the blanks about his move to Topeka.

"By the way, Sanjo, how did you like the burger?" asked Jack.

"It was very good Jack, ... with all of our jawboning, I worked up an appetite." "That's good. The burger was organic beef from the livestock on my ranch. It tastes good, and I believe that it's better for you than the mass-produced beef sold by large corporations that are fed with chemicals and corn, and pumped with growth hormones. So, I wanted to hear your opinion."

"You've been very busy Jack. I take it, we're going for a little spin." said Sanjo.

"Yeah, I flew the plane over this morning after we spoke. I was out at the ranch when you called, and was running a little short of time. I hope you don't mind. The ranch is only a short flight north and west, and I park the plane at the *Wamego Municipal Airport* when I'm up that way. I've got an old car parked at the airport that we can take to the ranch", he explained.

"Sounds good to me" Sanjo assured him. "It's not my first rodeo, so I'm up for a little adventure, I guess" trying to sound self-assured.

Sanjo pulled in next to the Quonset hut where Jack parked his Cessna, got out and locked his truck, then followed Jack through the single door of the hut to where the Cessna sat. Sanjo watched and asked a few questions as Jack walked around the plane to conduct a preflight inspection. Among other checks, he inspected the tires for proper inflation, the leading edges of the wings, prop, and vertical and horizontal stabilizers, the lock nut on the horizontal stabilizer, flaps, ailerons, and pitot tube inlet, oil and gas levels, secured gas caps, ignition wires, cowling pins, and checked the overall condition of the plane in general. Then he grabbed a small pail from the corner of the hut and drained the sump to make sure that there was no water in the gas. With that done, he raised the large overhead door to the front of the hut, and Sanjo helped him roll the Cessna out to the small ramp area in front of the hangar, … then, lowered the door behind him. Jack took another quick look around before they both jumped into the Cessna and secured their seatbelts. In the cockpit, he went through the checklist that was clipped to the dash.

CESSNA 170 CHECKLIST

PREFLIGHT
Check Battery Voltage
Check Fuel Gauge(s) & Fuel ON
All Electrical & Avionics Off
Flaps Down
Preflight Exterior
Check Oil Level (min.4 Qt., Max 7 Qt.)

BEFORE STARTING ENGINE
Check Tail Wheel Control (Crossed?)
Check Flaps Up.
Check Controls for Freedom
Fuel Valve to BOTH
Seat Tracks "Locked" & Seat Belts On

STARTING ENGINE
Carburetor Heat – COLD (In)
Throttle – ½ inch
Mixture – RICH (In)
Master Switch - ON
Ignition/Magnetos – ON BOTH
Prime if Required
CLEAR PROP
BRAKES ON then START ENGINE
CHECK OIL PRESSURE – (900 – 1000 RPM)
Lean Mixture

GPS, ATIS, Radio, Taxi Instructions.
BEFORE TAXI
Cabin Doors – Latched
Intercom – Verify its Working

Strobes - ON
Transponder – STANDBY (1200)
Communications Radio ON
Set Altimeter Per ATIS Information
Request TAXI from Ground Control

ENGINE RUNUP
BRAKES ON
Throttle – 1700 RPM
Magneto Check – (75/50)
Carburetor Heat (Look for Slight Drop)
Oil Pressure 30–40 psi/10 psi idle
Ammeter – Charging
Idle Engine (900-1000 RPM)

BEFORE TAKEOFF
Set DG
Mixture (Rich @ SL or Lean For "Max" Power)
Carb Heat (Verify Cold)
Set Trim to Takeoff Position
Fuel Valve to BOTH
Re-check Belts, Doors, & Windows
Transponder ON ALT (Altitude Encoder)
Switch to Tower Frequency

TAKEOFF
Flaps "0 for Normal" or 20 for Short Field
Full Throttle
Lift Tailwheel @ 25-30 MPH, Lift Off 60 MPH

CLIMB
Vx (F@0) = 76 MPH, Vx (F@20) = 67 MPH
Vy (@SL) = 89 MPH, Vy (@5K) = 83 MPH

CRUISE
Trim for Level Flight
Lean Mixture for "Max" power above 3000 Ft.
2450 RPM @ 5000 Ft. = 120 MPH @ 8 GPH

BEFORE LANDING
Fuel BOTH/Mixture "Rich"/Carb Heat ON
Full Throttle
Flaps (Best practice: Use only under 75 MPH
Then start approach 65-70 MPH for Landing

AFTER LANDING
CARB HEAT - OFF
FLAPS - UP
Transponder – OFF (If applicable)
Lean Mixture (If applicable)

SHUTDOWN & SECURING
Radio & Transponder - OFF
Strobes & Lights OFF
Mixture to Idle/Cutoff
Magnetos - OFF
Master - OFF
Keys Out and On Panel
Fuel to OFF position
CLOSE FLIGHT PLAN

Jack went through the whole checklist one item at a time, but quickly, since he knew the list by heart, and had just flown the plane earlier that morning. He recorded the tach time in his log book, checked the altimeter for the correct barometric pressure according to the field elevation at 1,078 feet ASL, then set the mixture rich, carb heat cold, made sure the fuel valves were switched to ON, primed the throttle, and turned the Master Switch to ON. He checked the area around the plane once again, then yelled, "Clear", turned the key, and brought the engine speed up to about 1100 RPM idle after it started. With a quick check of the list again, he observed the oil pressure, then tuned the radio to a frequency of 121.7 for the airport Ground Control, as he spiked the mike.

"Forbes Field Ground Control, this is Cessna two-eight-four-seven Whiskey at the south end of the field with the numbers", he said. "Taxi for takeoff".

"Roger, Cessna 47 Whiskey, taxi to runway two-one and hold short of the runway" cracked the reply. "Switch to tower frequency 120.8 when in position."

"Roger, 47 Whiskey" replied Jack. Then he gently pushed the throttle forward and using his foot pedals to steer the plane, proceeded to taxi toward runway 21 looking for the windsock, while Sanjo watched and listened. When he arrived at the runway, he held short, then turned the plane left at a slight angle to Runway 21, into the wind, and went through his run-up following the 'Before Takeoff' instructions on his Cessna checklist. He checked the ailerons for freedom of movement, pulled and released 10, then 20 degrees of flap, rechecked that the fuel valve was switched to ON, increased the throttle to read 1700 RPM on the tach, checked the left and right magnetos, and carb heat cold for the correct RPM drop, as well as the gauges again. Then he switched to the tower frequency at 120.8 Hz to prepare for takeoff. There was no traffic in sight, so he was pretty sure that the tower would clear him quickly.

"Forbes Field Tower, Cessna two-eight-four-seven Whiskey, holding short Runway Two One, ready for takeoff" he said.

""Roger, 47 Whiskey. You're cleared for takeoff, Runway Two-One". With that, Jack turned the plane south on to the active runway, made another quick check of the gauges, then gently pushed the throttle toward the firewall accelerating down the runway, lifting off at about 65 MPH, and climbing out at 75 MPH. Upon reaching traffic altitude and the end of the field, he made a standard left turn heading south as he continued to climb toward 4,500 feet on the altimeter. As he continued to check for traffic all around, he turned the plane north toward *Wamego Municipal Airport* and the ranch. When they reached altitude they signaled a 'thumbs up' to each other and continued to enjoy the Topeka landscape that surrounded them. As Sanjo watched the Kansas farmland from above, he thought, "It's not a job, it's an adventure". He smiled broadly, then remembered *Pernicious*, as the last *Blind Tiger* continued to work its magic.

Jack's ranch was located only about 20 minutes flying time northwest of Forbes Field, but as they approached their destination, Jack could see that Sanjo was enjoying himself, so he decided to show him a bit more of the Kansas countryside, pointing out a few local landmarks within a 15 mile radius of the ranch. At one point, when he had the plane flying straight and level, he asked Sanjo to take the stick while giving him some basic flying lessons. He made some gradual 15 degree turns, showed him how to work the pedals and controls, and pointed out the standard instruments. Then he a made a few basic maneuvers like 'turns about a point' and a "chandelle' to give him a better feel of flying, building his confidence. Overall, they were in the air for almost an hour before Jack decided to make his final approach to Wamego.

About 10 miles out, Jack set the radio at 122.9 Hz for Wamego Unicom to notify other air traffic in the area. Then he set course for the left downwind leg of runway 17, checking traffic and entering the pattern north of the river as he descended.

"Wamego Unicom, this is Cessna two-eight-four-seven Whiskey, left downwind for runway one-seven, landing, over". At about 1,000 feet AGL he put the fuel mixture at rich, pulled carburetor heat, notified traffic that he was entering his base leg, and then turned for final approach a couple of minutes later as he pulled 10 degrees of flap. The landing was 'picture perfect' as he rolled to a stop at the end of the runway, made a U-turn, and taxied back up to the terminal and the tie-down area on the ramp. Since they were both sailors, they knew how to tie a hitch. They tied down the Cessna, placed chocks around the wheels, and then walked over to Jack's old '89 Bimmer 325i coupe that was parked near one of the hangars. They were the only two souls for as far as the eye could see. Sanjo actually felt good to be back on the ground again and in a car, but he thanked Jack for the flying lesson, and the tour of the Topeka landscape.

"It was my pleasure Sanjo, I hope you enjoyed it as much as I did." Then he put the Bimmer in 1st gear, and like a high school kid, peeled out of the gravel airport road onto the adjacent Red Top road, shifting gears and racing west past the cornfields all the way to the ranch.

Sanjo's first impression of the ranch was that it was Jack's Monticello, minus the slave labor. The main house was a converted ranch house that Jack had modified to his own design. In both the front and back of the house he had added immense porches with columns, which made the entire structure appear grandiose. Jack called the porches his "Porticos". He had also added a library on the east end of the house, and a matching study on the west end to accommodate guests, as well as give him more privacy when he needed it. He was a modern-day Thomas Jefferson with countless contemporary gadgets; some of which, he had developed himself. Many of the devices that he had made were assembled using a fastener that he had developed and patented. The only hand tool required to put any structure together was a small drill motor, and one size drill bit. The fastener was then used to hold the structural members in compression using a ¼ turn cam action of the fastener. With them, he constructed housings for his remote generator, solar panels to generate electricity, a weathervane, wind turbines and augers of various designs, and many other unique devices that allowed him to be more independent. A lesson he had learned in the Navy.

On his ranch, Jack kept about 20 dairy cows, some beef cattle, as well as the usual chickens, pigs, a couple of horses, and two goats. He also raised about 100 acres of corn, as well as some wheat. His foreman Ray Forbes, was like a brew master for milk. He took care of the cows, made Kiefer for their personal use (as well as for local sale), and even made some cheese. The milk truck came every other day to keep the commerce moving. Jack kept some of the raw milk for himself because, like the fermented Kiefer, Jack believed that it was healthier than store-bought milk, and it helped his immune system. Ray also managed all of their part time help to keep everything ship shape. Ray was also quite handy and had helped Jack to construct the additions to his ranch house, as well as the small pavilions on the property that served as quarters for laborers, as well as observation platforms overlooking the land. Actually, Ray pretty much ran the place, and mainly looked to Jack for advice when he had questions. Jack saw himself as more of a coach and a strategic planner than a grunt, and having Ray around the ranch gave Jack more time to tinker with his toys.

"Sanjo, are ya ready for a chilled *Holy Grail Pale Ale*?" asked Jack.

"Sure Jack! The *Blind Tiger* disappeared after that last chandelle. I prefer the light colored beer anyway, ... I just liked the sound of the *Blind Tiger*", he confessed. With that, they popped the tops on a couple of cold beers as Jack walked him around the ranch showing him some of his achievements. Jack's Irish Setter 'Natasha' followed them around the farm. There were also some cats, but they kept to themselves around the barn.

A couple of hours after the tour, and after they had finished their dinner, *Pernicious* showed up at the ranch with her friend *Enchanté*. They looked like they could have been sisters, except that *Enchanté* had more Irish looks, and slightly reddish hair with a few freckles. The two of them had finished work at the *Jack of Clubs*, and were in the mood for a little diversion and some relaxation. They liked driving out to the ranch because it took them away from Topeka where they were less likely to run into the local clientele, and could behave more *'Au Naturel'*. Their real names were Carol Mulhaney and Sarah Reid, but they enjoyed a level of make believe when it worked to their advantage. They brought with them a bottle of wine and a little 'stash' to help lift their spirits.

Pernicious introduced her friend to Sanjo, since she was planning to spend some extra time with Jack. *Enchanté* already knew Jack from the club, and had seen Sanjo earlier in the day, but hadn't yet met him. They decided to pop the cork on the bottle of wine they brought since they had enjoyed enough of the pale ale. Here, they used their real names since there was no need for disguise, and they enjoyed hearing about each other's personal history and how they had all come to settle in a place like Topeka. Carol mostly listened, since she was learning too. She was quite fond of Jack, but really wanted to know more about his past. Like, how did a kid from Rockford, Minnesota end up in Topeka, Kansas? What was the driving force, and were there any skeletons in the closet? Of course, they also enjoyed Jack and Sanjo's stories about their time in the Navy and how that experience shaped their lives. Contrary to popular opinion, strippers really can be smart people.

Then Carol asked, "So Jack, how did you end up in Topeka?"

To his chagrin, he had never actually revealed the story to many people prior to that day. So, Sarah just got lucky because she was with Carol at the time. But it didn't matter; Jack was eager to get it off his chest. As is often the case, it involved a girl that Jack had spent some time with a very long time ago. They were both much younger at the time, and the girl was from Jack's hometown of Rockford, Minnesota. To make a long story short, the girl had become pregnant at a very inconvenient time in their lives, and after much agony, misery, and grief, the girl left her home and family, and traveled south to Kansas to live with relatives until she could decide how to remedy the situation. Since the girl had been raised in a family that was adamantly against abortion, she felt immense shame and pressure, and decided that it would be best to leave town for a while. Jack was believed to have been the father. After the baby was born, she kept it for a while after leaving the hospital, but soon decided that it was too heavy a burden to suffer at such a young age. She decided to put the baby up for adoption in Kansas, made certain that the child was placed in a good home, then quietly returned to Minnesota to resume her life. This always bothered Jack. In fact, it was one of the reasons that he had joined the Navy rather than remain in his hometown of Rockford. So, after spending almost two decades in the Middle East, in part running away from himself, he found that he was drawn back to Kansas, and Topeka in particular, to try to come to terms with his actions, as well as pursue some peace, happiness, and prosperity. The issue was still unresolved in his mind.

"Wow, Jack! I don't know what to say" said Carol. "I had no idea that this was bothering you".

"Well, it's not something that I'm proud of Carol. As Sanjo can tell you, our ship's motto in the Navy was *Judicemur Agendo*, which is latin for *'Let us be judged by our deeds'*, he said. "Maybe there's some divine reason that I was assigned to that particular ship".

"Yeah, Jack. I remember now" said Sanjo. "You had also written a poem called *'Down On The Farm'* during our first deployment when you wrote the other poems. And, I recall that it had a similar theme. Am I correct?"

"Yeah, that's about right." said Jack. "Writing poems was good therapy for me, and it helped me clear my head as we were counting time".

"OK, Jack, let's hear it" said Carol, knowing that Jack would probably welcome an opportunity to demonstrate his right brain creativity.

"Sure. It's called *'Down on the Farm'* he said, as he recited the poem from memory.

Down on the Farm

I didn't want to settle down, It wasn't in my plan.
But now I don't know where to go, Since I've hit fertile land.

She came upon me softly, Sort of snuck up from behind. We spent some time
together, Then she coyly blew my mind.

She said "I've a surprise for you, I think you ought to hear!"
I think that I am pregnant. How do you like that dear?"

I nearly lost my little head, My mind went sort of blank.
My dreams sailed by before me, My dreamboat passed, and sank.

"What is your plan of action?" I asked in plain remorse.
She looked at me in disbelief. "To marry you, of course!"

I thought that I could leave her. I started to regress.
But, I knew too well that she must have My true name, and address.

I don't really want to marry her, I don't know if I can.
But now I don't know where to go, Since I've hit fertile land.

Jaak - 1973, South China Seas

Flight deck to Flight Deck, 'Flint' versus 'Kitty Hawk', South Pacific

Down on the Farm, Philippines, Between Subic Bay and Clark Air Base

"Whoa, that's pretty chicken shit!" shot Carol. "But it may help to explain why you bought a ranch in Kansas. Did that really happen?"

"Like, I said Carol, it wasn't one of my finer moments. All I can say is that, many of us make mistakes. It's part of the learning process. With some mistakes, we end up making payments for the rest of our lives." Jack replied somewhat sheepishly.

"Well, I can say first hand, that many of the sailors on our ship were running from something" said Sanjo, "including the law. And, I'm sure that many of them made similar mistakes in their early years" he said, trying to console Jack as well as back him up. "Let's hear another poem, Jack. Perhaps, something a little more light-hearted".

"OK, since you enjoyed the flight up here today Sanjo, here's one that I wrote after our first deployment, when we returned to San Francisco. I wrote it about flying because I used to go out to the local airport on liberty, to Buchanan Field, and watch the planes take off and land. It's called *Light Wings*" he replied. Then he recited;

Light Wings

White wings Light wings
These are all the right things.
They are what are on my mind
I think about them most the time.

Tight wings,
Taut with canvas stretched.
Lighter than air
Very fair

Floating over the runway
With the greatest care,
And then they flare.

Nothing else makes much sense
As I watch the plane's descent's
The joy I feel is immense
As I watch them fly.

Many trees are standing bare
In the breeze of the warm fall air
And I haven't a single care,
As I watch them fly.

White wings
Light wings
These are all the right things
Kite strings

Bright things
Of them I am aware.

Jaak - 1974, Buchanan Field, Concord, California

"Bravo!" said Carol. "You know, you really are special, Jack", she said, as she gave him a wink and a tender glance. With that, Jack and Sanjo got up and moved from the kitchen to the living room. Carol and Sarah stepped out onto the back Portico for about 10 minutes to converse, look over the ranch, and light up a joint. Jack and Sanjo remained in the living room since they had no desire to climb to that level of relaxation. When the girls returned they began to get chatty again, and settled in for a spell.

To set the mood, Jack inserted a disk into the CD player that contained songs from some of his favorite artists including Bob Dylan, the Rolling Stones, Pink Floyd, the Doors, some country music that featured a little bit of fiddle and guitar, and even some Spanish songs from Linda Ronstadt. His stereo speakers had been purchased at the PX in the Philippines and were left over from his Navy days. As the evening wore on, the conversation rambled like a steel ball in a pachinko game, and they learned a lot more about one another. Jack and Carol later retired to another room, as Sanjo and Sarah got to know each other a little better in the living room. The two girls slipped away around two in the morning, since they had to work the next day. Sanjo found another room with a rack of his own, and the two of them mustered again at around 9:30 the next morning.

Sanjo and Jack awoke to greet a rainy day, and grumpy stomachs. They showered and shaved, flossed between their teeth, dried between their toes, got dressed, then met each other in the kitchen for some scrambled eggs, toast, bacon and orange juice. They poured some hot black coffee, and then moved from the kitchen to the back portico to watch the rain.

"Looks like we won't be flying today" said Jack. "I'll take you into town in the Bimmer to get your truck, and we can rendezvous back here after I've taken care of a few chores in town. How does that sound Sanjo?"

"That sounds good Jack. I need to check my messages and check in at home, but then I'm good to go. I'd like to stay here in Topeka for a couple of days, but then I plan to head back up to Des Moines for my meeting on Tuesday before heading back to Duluth", he said.

"That's not a problem Sanjo. You're welcome to stay as long as you like. I'm sure that we both have plenty to do, and can stay out of each other's hair until we need to reconnoiter again" said Jack.

"Perfect", replied Sanjo. "Let me know when you want to go to town, and I'll work around your schedule."

"OK. Let's plan to head out in about half an hour" he said.

THE TROUBLE WITH TOPEKA

"I woke, she fled and day brought back my night."
-Edgar Allen Poe

On the way back to Sanjo's truck in Jack's 'Bimmer', Jack asked Sanjo whether he had enjoyed the night before, and his thoughts about Carol (*Pernicious*) and Sarah, (*Enchanté*).

"Well, it was quite a thrill", said Sanjo. "A bit more than I bargained for, but certainly entertaining! I especially liked the dance set they did in your living room after the music cranked up, as they began to get a little buzz on. I haven't seen dancing like that since the *California Club* in the Philippines. It really took me back to our Navy days. I also hadn't expected them to completely strip like that in your front room" he said. "And, I was very impressed with Sarah's flexibility. She must do a lot of stretching exercises." he added.

"Yeah, the two of them can get pretty wound up and exotic when they want to! Jack said with a laugh. It's one of the reasons that I invested in the *Jack of Clubs*". "It takes me back to the days when we were free, white, and single!"

"You're still free, white, and single Jack! And to top that, you appear to be making more money, with more independence, than you've had in your entire life! What's not to like? That's gotta be worth the price of admission alone in my book!

"Yeah, as I said before, life is good, if we can make it last." "Wha' chu mean, 'We', kimosabe?" he asked.

"Well, I mean Carol and I" he continued, being a bit evasive. "I've messed up so many relationships in the past, I don't want to push this one too hard. In fact, I think that I'm better off just leaving the whole thing alone. But, you know how women are! They like to tie you down. Then all the fizzle turns into a puddle, and dries up!" he confided.

"Interesting metaphor, Jack. But she's half your age. How's that gonna work? I mean, we're not really made to run until the wheels fall off" he counseled. "But it's your life, and your decision. Do you like your life as a sovereign individual?

I'd say that you're already 'giving back to the community' with that little gem of a place you've got going at the airport."

"The plane, or the club?, asked Jack with a grin.

"You know what I mean Jack. And on top of that, you probably do a lot of cash business at the club, which can help your free cash flow situation, if you know what I mean."

"Sure. Another reason for investing" he said. "Why give it all to the government when companies like GM, GE, and big oil don't pay any taxes at all?"

"That's right! They keep sticking it to the little guy, while we bust our ass trying to make it month to month" said Sanjo.

"Well yes, we've had this discussion before" said Jack. "But I'm no longer in a situation where I have to worry about expenses month to month. I'm more concerned with these clowns in government crashing the whole system, then devaluing the dollar like they did in 1933 under Roosevelt" Jack retorted.

"No need" said Sanjo. They've been doing it all along, by just printing more money. That's why a gallon of gas is four bucks today, when it was forty cents when we were kids. It's all priced in. It isn't that the price of gas is going up, it's that the value of the dollar is going down, since there's nothing backing it up but bullshit. The US government went off the gold standard under Nixon in '71, and now it's a race to the bottom with all western currencies. We're all going Greek!" he continued.

"I mean, nothing is real, it's just what we make it, we're making the motions, while we really just fake it!"

"Isn't that right?" said Sanjo. "Chu got it mahn!" said Jack.

"When will it all end, this follow the leader?" Sanjo went on.

"Good point!" said Jack. "But, that's enough of that shit. Now I have to go listen to some relaxation tapes just to get my head back on a frequency of 7.83 Hertz".

"Or, you could just go back to the club and look up Carol" said Sanjo.

When they arrived back at *Forbes Field*, Jack dropped Sanjo off at his truck, checked that the hangar was secure, then said "Ok, Sanjo, I'll see you back at the ranch later on", and waved goodbye. "OK, Jack. Keep your nose clean, and stay out of trouble" Sanjo advised, as they parted ways.

But Jack hadn't told Sanjo the whole story. As it happens, very little was actually 'real'. Rather, it was just 'Jack making it up' as he went along. Or, as Jack might say, 'improvisation'. Jack felt that one often needed to change horses in mid-stream if the initial plan ran into problems, or the situation called for adjustments. When it came to investments, Jack never liked to use his own money, and he had met some pretty savvy, but shady characters over the years while traveling throughout the world. In fact, when it came to setting up the club, Jack had actually met with several "outside investors" to put up cash to close the deal with the local bank. The 'outside investors' were not only from outside of the country, but in the eyes of a few, also outside of US law. And, some of them spoke pretty good Russian. There were more people hanging around the *Jack of Clubs* on any given day than just local businessmen and bikers. And much of that "free cash flow" found its way back to various people that came into the club rather frequently, that also had an interest in protecting 'their' investments. Those same people had placed similar clubs at airports all around the country, along with pawnshops, quick cash outlets, porn shops, and drug and prostitution rings, that may have also been involved in money laundering, extortion, human trafficking, and organized crime. The free cash flow had a way of helping them get into plenty of other 'free cash flow' businesses that helped to grease the wheels with their favorite judges and politicians, and help lubricate the underground economy. In fact, if one 'followed the money', one might find that a lot of it went full circle from the clubs, to middle men, to the pawn shops, to politicians, to community organizers, to casinos, to bigger banks, to numbered accounts in the Caymans, Switzerland, Liechtenstein, Singapore, and Panama, to gun running and drug trafficking operations, covert military operations, Central Banks, the Middle East, big government, and again back to community organizers and politicians, then back to the middle men, and back to the clubs. Like Jack said, 'we are all connected', and like the old days, when Jack ran the plan, everything worked like a well- greased rail.

The same people that had helped Jack with some quick cash for investments also had broader plans for Jack. And, the girls at the club hadn't just arrived out of nowhere or for that matter, from Topeka. In fact, they were all part of a more complex system. So, although Sanjo had admired *Enchanté's* moves the night before, he didn't quite know all of the elements of the relationship, and the wily web being woven like a fine Persian rug.

Back in town, while checking out the local scenery, Sanjo called his wife Marissa back in Duluth to let her know that he had arrived in Topeka safely, and would be staying with his pal 'Jack' for a few days at the ranch. He told her about the plane ride in Jack's Cessna taildragger, all of the toys that Jack had accumulated in Kansas, as well as the wonderful weather they were having. He promised to keep in touch, but that he might be sidetracked for the next couple of days as he visited with Jack, attended his meeting in Des Moines, and gradually worked his way back to Duluth. Marissa assured him that everything was fine back home, told him that she loved him, and reminded him to drive carefully, and to watch for deer. He assured her that he would.

After that, Sanjo drove around Topeka looking for a place to connect to the internet. He found a Starbucks coffee shop in a small roadside strip mall on the northwest side of town near the Topeka Golf Course, north of Sherwood Lake. He grabbed the rucksack out of his truck and went in and ordered a tall latte, parked himself in a corner, and connected his laptop to their Wifi network. He spent a good hour checking and answering his e-mail messages, and exploring Topeka vicariously through the miracle of the world-wide-web. He learned that the Topeka legislature had a House Bill 2107 called the *Community Defense Act* that had been proposed to "regulate the hours of operation and the inside configuration of sexually oriented businesses" in Topeka. The bill "passed with an overwhelmingly majority in the House of Representatives" the prior year by a 96-23 vote. As he surfed the web for additional information and read a few related blogs, he discovered that there were as many people against the bill, as there were supporting it. Related articles had titles like "Nude dancing bill hits bump", and "Lap dancing may grind to a halt". Yet, the businesses were all operating, and the bill was in limbo. So, who was in control, he wondered?

As the afternoon wore on, Sanjo left Starbucks and decided to explore the area around the *Topeka Golf Course* and *Sherwood Lake* to get a better feel of the area, and to see how it compared with other areas of the country. Pretty standard, he thought. Like many communities, there seemed to be a good side of town, and a less than good side of town. But as far as Sanjo was concerned, there were also two economies; one economy for people that operate within the system, and who pay taxes, ... and another economy for people that operate outside the system, and don't pay taxes. So, it depended upon which side of the fence that one was situated. Sanjo didn't like paying taxes any more than the next guy, and he believed that people were severely overtaxed relative to what citizens get for their taxes. In addition, he believed that some taxes were in fact, unconstitutional since in the 16th Amendment, Article I, Section 8 of *The United States Constitution* they only call for certain items to be taxed. He also believed that the country should pass an amendment calling for a balanced national budget, and that the US Congress should by law, not be allowed to spend money beyond the agreed annual budget. But of course, the elected representatives were always going to do what was best for them, as well as find creative ways to circumvent the law to suit their individual interpretations, and perceived needs. The 16th Amendment to the US Constitution, Article 1, Section 8 actually states;

Section 8

1: The Congress shall have Power To lay and collect Taxes, Duties, Imposts and Excises, to pay the Debts and provide for the common Defence and general Welfare of the United States; but all Duties, Imposts and Excises shall be uniform throughout the United States;

2: To borrow Money on the credit of the United States;

3: To regulate Commerce with foreign Nations, and among the several States, and with the Indian Tribes;

4: To establish an uniform Rule of Naturalization, and uniform Laws on the subject of Bankruptcies throughout the United States;

5: To coin Money, regulate the Value thereof, and of foreign Coin, and fix the Standard of Weights and Measures;

6: To provide for the Punishment of counterfeiting the Securities and current Coin of the United States;

7: To establish Post Offices and post Roads;

8: To promote the Progress of Science and useful Arts, by securing for limited Times to Authors and Inventors the exclusive Right to their respective Writings and Discoveries;

9: To constitute Tribunals inferior to the Supreme Court;

10: To define and punish Piracies and Felonies committed on the high Seas, and Offences against the Law of Nations;

11: To declare War, grant Letters of Marque and Reprisal, and make Rules concerning Captures on Land and Water;

12: To raise and support Armies, but no Appropriation of Money to that Use shall be for a longer Term than two Years;

13: To provide and maintain a Navy;

14: To make Rules for the Government and Regulation of the land and naval Forces;

15: To provide for calling forth the Militia to execute the Laws of the Union, suppress Insurrections and repel Invasions;

16: To provide for organizing, arming, and disciplining, the Militia, and for governing such Part of them as may be employed in the Service of the United States, reserving to the States respectively, the Appointment of the Officers, and the Authority of training the Militia according to the discipline prescribed by Congress;

17: To exercise exclusive Legislation in all Cases whatsoever, over such District (not exceeding ten Miles square) as may, by Cession of particular States, and the Acceptance of Congress, become the Seat of the Government of the United States, and to exercise like Authority over all Places purchased by the Consent of the Legislature of the State in which the Same shall be, for the Erection of Forts, Magazines, Arsenals, dock-Yards, and other needful Buildings;--And

18: To make all Laws which shall be necessary and proper for carrying into Execution the foregoing Powers, and all other Powers vested by this Constitution in the Government of the United States, or in any Department or Officer thereof.

As a point of contention, from *Wikipedia*, it states;

To raise revenue to fund the Civil War, Congress introduced the income tax through the Revenue Act of 1861.[3] It levied a flat tax of 3% on annual income above $800, which was equivalent to $20,693 in today's money.[4] This act was replaced the following year with the Revenue Act of 1862, which levied a graduated tax of 3–5% on income above $600 (worth $13,968 today[4]) and specified a termination of income taxation in 1866.

So, what happened to the termination of the tax in 1866, and the 3-5% on income above $600 (worth $13,968 today)? The last time he looked, it appeared to Sanjo that the Federal income tax was closer to a tipping point of 35% of the money he earned. So, it appeared to him that the Federal Government was not much better than the Mafia; in fact, with all of their covert activities, it might be argued that they were indeed worse. Obviously, the general population was still overtaxed, and government too large, since a current accounting showing some of the taxes levied today, as outlined in an article written by Charlie Reese in his final column for the Orlando [Florida] Sentinel, listed the following current taxes paid by Americans, which hadn't existed 100 years ago. They included;

Accounts Receivable Tax Building Permit Tax CDL license Tax Cigarette Tax
Corporate Income Tax Dog License Tax Excise Taxes
Federal Income Tax
Federal Unemployment Tax (FUTA) Fishing License Tax
Food License Tax Fuel Permit Tax
Gasoline Tax (currently 44.75 cents per gallon) Gross Receipts Tax
Hunting License Tax Inheritance Tax Inventory Tax
IRS Interest Charges IRS Penalties (tax on top of tax) Liquor Tax
Luxury Taxes Marriage License Tax Medicare Tax Personal Property Tax
Property Tax Real Estate Tax
Service Charge Tax Social Security Tax Road Usage Tax Recreational Vehicle Tax Sales Tax
School Tax
State Income Tax
State Unemployment Tax (SUTA) Telephone Federal Excise Tax
Telephone Federal Universal Service Fee Tax Telephone Federal, State and Local Surcharge Taxes Telephone Minimum Usage Surcharge Tax

Telephone Recurring and Nonrecurring Charges Tax Telephone State and Local Tax
Telephone Usage Charge Tax Utility Taxes
Vehicle License Registration Tax Vehicle Sales Tax
Watercraft Registration Tax Well Permit Tax
Workers Compensation Tax http://www.zerohedge.com/news/2016-04-03/land-free

Of course, the list didn't include the extra taxes that Sanjo had just paid on his last hotel bill during his current business trip. And, on top of that, the government had purchased or confiscated much of the good land, turned it into State and National Parks, and now charged a fee to get in. So, Sanjo could understand why there might be two sides to Topeka, as well as two sides to the argument about taxes, which made people think about which side of the fence they preferred to sit on.

In any case, Sanjo could see that the trouble with Topeka wasn't going to solve itself any time soon. Since it was getting late, and he hadn't heard from Jack, he decided to take another ride over to the *Jack of Clubs* to see what kind of trouble he could find for himself. The events of the previous evening were still pirouetting in his head as he remembered the performance by his two newest best friends, *Pernicious* (Carol), and *Enchanté* (Sarah). It was beginning to get dark, so Sanjo reckoned that Jack might have gotten sidetracked at the club for longer than expected. It was a short ride across town, and he began to develop a thirst for another refreshing *Holy Grail Pale Ale*.

As he pulled into the parking lot of the club, there were many more cars, trucks, and bikes than had been there the previous afternoon. He decided that it was a good sign since it would help Jack's business. He also spotted Jack's black '89 Bimmer, so he knew that he had come to the right place. The large neon lights lit the parking lot as he walked through the front door. This time, a scantily attired gal stood behind the front counter requesting a $5 dollar cover charge to enter. He smiled politely, paid the cover, walked through another door back to the raised platform at the rear of the club, and pulled up a chair at the table where he had sat the day before. The club was crowded, and he observed that a few guys now occupied the bench seats where they were being entertained by dancers.

How special, he thought, as he tried to adjust his eyes to the darkness amid the flashing lights, and louder music. On this occasion there were two girls dancing in different corners of the club as a number of other dancers walked around talking to customers and serving drinks. As his eyes adjusted to the low light, he looked around to see whether he could find Jack. What he found was his new best friend *Enchanté* (Sarah), sitting next to a customer talking her book. After a period of time, she looked his way, leaned over to say something to the customer, then got up and walked over to Sanjo's table, and sat down beside him.

"Hello Sarah. I mean *Enchanté*." he apologized. "I forgot that you're working".

"Yes, I am working Sanjo, thanks for remembering".

"Can I get you something to drink? Are you looking for Jack?" she asked. "Well, yeah. I saw his 'Bimmer' outside, and we agreed to meet later, so I thought I'd come in and relax, watch the local talent, and have another one of those full bodied *Holy Grail Pale Ales*", he said.

"Sure" she said. "Let me get you one" as she signaled to a girl near her, and asked her to bring a cold *Holy Grail Pale Ale* right over. Then, she turned again to Sanjo, and smiled.

"I really enjoyed our time together last night Sanjo" she said affectionately. "Well, yeah. I enjoyed it too! It was a very nice performance that you and *Pernicious* put on," he said. "But I have to ask, do you do a lot of stretching exercises, or are you just naturally flexible like that?" he asked.

"So you liked our dance," she replied with a smile. "What's not to like?" he asked.

"Well I'm glad you liked it! We had fun".

"As you said a minute ago, in the club here, I'm working, so I have to get as many dances in as I can during a normal shift. Would you like me to dance for you now?" she asked. And at that moment, the other girl arrived back at the table and placed a *Holy Grail Pale Ale* on the table in front of him.

"Well, yes, I think that I'd enjoy that *Enchanté*."he said. "What's it going to set me back?

"Twenty dollars for a single dance," she said, "or, thirty dollars for two". "Well, since we're killing time here anyway *Enchanté*, let's go for the double" he said.

"That's good Sanjo, thanks. Then, I'm allowed to spend more time with you. If you can order a drink for me after I dance, I can spend even more time with you before I have to go sit with another customer", she said.

"Terrific!" he said, as she began to go through her routine, and became even more up close and personal than the night before. About halfway through the first dance routine, Sanjo could feel himself becoming aroused as he began to rapidly sip his beer, and question whether he had done the right thing. But then the effects of the *Holy Grail Pale Ale* began to work its magic and he decided to just shut-up and enjoy the entertainment. It sure beat anything that was currently on TV. After she finished her two dances, Sanjo ordered her a drink, and when the lemonade arrived, she spent another ten minutes or so with him before saying "Thank you, Sanjo. I'll see you later at Jack's ranch", then walked over to another table to entertain more customers.

When he could refocus, Sanjo looked towards the bar, saw *Pernicious* talking to Jack, and watched as Jack looked over his way and waved. Sanjo acknowledged, then ordered another *Holy Grail Pale Ale*. Also at the bar, talking to Jack were two better-dressed gentlemen with a rather foreign appearance. At least, to Sanjo, they didn't look like they were from the neighborhood. Maybe it was just his imagination, he decided. Or maybe it was the beer. He continued to watch the dancing girls.

Sanjo ordered one of their special 'organic beef' *Hungry Jack* burgers and another beer as he passed the time. Then as 8:00 PM rolled around, Sanjo had had about enough. He walked up to the bar, found Jack, said hello, then told him that he was a bit tired and informed him that he would meet him back at the ranch. Jack understood, apologized for not having more time, and told Sanjo that he would meet him at the house later. With that, Sanjo found the exit, his truck keys, and the cool evening parking lot. He was pretty sure of the way out to the ranch, but got turned around a couple of times as he headed northwest. Nevertheless, he found Red Top road past the *Wamego Municipal Airport* and made his way to the ranch. Ray Forbes greeted him when Sanjo drove up the driveway as he was coming back to the house from the barn after some nightly chores.

"Just go on inside and make yourself comfortable" Ray instructed.

Sanjo said "Thanks, Ray" and did just that. Suddenly, he felt exhausted from a long day; so he found the room and the bed that he had slept in the night before, took off his shoes, put on some pajama bottoms, laid back, and put his head on the pillow. Within a couple of minutes he was out like a light.

At around 2:30 AM, Sanjo heard Jack's Bimmer racing up Red Top road and into the long gravel driveway of the ranch. Another car followed right behind him, and he heard their car doors slam as they got out laughing and carrying on as they approached the porch. It was Jack, with his new best friends, Carol and Sarah. They were winding down from a night on the town, and were now ready for a little more fun. Sanjo was glad that he had just gotten about five hours of deep sleep. He felt like he had just been rousted for the "mid-shitter" (midnight) watch, like during his old Navy days, and was ready for some "mid-rats" (midnight rations on the mess decks). The three of them found Sanjo resting on his rack and encouraged him to join them in the living room for a little more music, and a nightcap. Sanjo obliged trying to shake the sleep from his head as they handed him a shot of Courvoisier. The two girls were still in their club outfits except for the cowgirl boots that had replaced their high heels, and were ready for some action as they removed their boots and began to dance to the Country Western music that Jack had quickly put into the CD player; and, the living room quickly came alive.

"I think I'm getting too old for this shit" Sanjo scowled, as the girls cranked up the volume, and turned down the lights. The girls obviously had another little buzz going as they both grabbed Jack, and the three of them began to dance, while Sanjo just sat on the couch and watched in wonder. When Jack had danced enough, he lowered the volume a tad, then sat down in a chair in the far corner of room, as Carol continued dancing. A moment later, she ambled over to Jack and began to give him a lap dance. Not to be outdone, Sarah slowly danced over to where Sanjo was seated, and gave him a repeat performance of her earlier dance routine, only this time shedding bits of her clothing as she worked her magic. He began to feel the effects of the Courvoisier at about the same time that she noticed a prominent protuberance in his cotton pajamas, and that's when she went down on him, making her performance all the more pleasurable. "Is that a rocket in your pocket, or are you just glad to see me", she swooned?

One of the last things that Sanjo remembered was gently sliding down the front edge of the couch to maneuver himself into a more tactical position for a close-in inspection as she delicately danced above his head, and he recalled the announcement heard every evening over the 1MC loudspeaker system aboard ship; "Taps, taps, lights out, all hands heave into your own racks; Dinner for cooks, mess-cooks, and oncoming watch-standers. Muster restricted men with the duty master at arms, at the master at arms office; Now, taps". Then he went down for more mid-rats. The party continued for another hour before Jack and Carol retired to another room, and Sarah pulled Sanjo back to his. With all the excitement, and extracurricular activity, they were soon all sound asleep in their respective spaces, as the night wore away. A fresh and brilliant sunny day burst upon them around 9:30 AM the following morning.

Sarah and Sanjo, Carol and Jack, all awoke in their rooms to greet a cheery new day, but with multiple grumpy stomachs. They showered and shaved, flossed between their teeth, dried between their toes, got dressed, then met in the kitchen for some French toast, assorted fruits, croissants, bacon, and grapefruit juice that Carol and Sarah whipped up. They chatted and smirked, fondled and stroked each other for a time, then poured some hot black coffee, and moved to the porch to salute the sunshine and plan their day. Since it was Thursday, the girls had the day off. Since it was sunny, the girls wanted Jack to take them for a plane ride. And since the plane was still tied down at *Wamego Municipal Airport* just down the road from the ranch, Jack agreed that it would be a fine way to begin their day. With that, Sarah hopped into the truck with Sanjo, and Carol rode in the BMW with Jack down Red Top road, and over to *Wamego Municipal Airport*.

It was a beautiful morning and they were all feeling quite relaxed. Since the Cessna 170 was a "four-seater", Jack could fit everyone in at once. Therefore, Sanjo and Sarah sat in the back seat, as Jack took the left front seat at the controls, and Carol rode shotgun. *Wamego Airport* was magnificent in the morning light. The field adjacent to the runway was immersed in a magical light with sparkling dewdrops in the green grass, and light beams streaming through broken cumulus clouds. There was no one else around. Jack went through his checklist, announced his intentions on Unicom frequency 122.9 Hertz, pointed the plane down the runway into the wind, and sailed into the air. It was a lovely flight. He performed some of the same general maneuvers that he had shown Sanjo a few days before, and they all got a thrill out of the ride. After about 45 minutes, Jack returned to the field, set the plane down gently in the cool, crisp morning air, and they all returned to the ranch. All in all, a wonderful beginning to a delightful day. They were awakened, they were refreshed, they felt awareness, and they felt love, and a new vibration.

"Learning to fly is something that I've always wanted to do" said Sanjo.

Back at the ranch they all parted ways, kissed goodbye, and separated into their own routines for the day. The next three days and nights unfolded in a similar manner with all of the fun and frolic, but without the plane rides. Maybe it was just the Spring air and the country pollen; Maybe it was a reflection of their Navy days and a yearning for their past; Or, maybe it was the beginning of something bigger. Either way, they had read Sanjo's book, and were planning their next play. There were many more moves to make as their futures unfolded, and the trouble in Topeka would not easily go away.

Big Coke Bottle, Philippines, 1975

Temptress

Curvaceous thighs, smoke spiraled highs, Money hungry friars.
Cherry pie, ham on rye, Sink into the mire.

A futile try, the devils' lie Cried to take him higher.
A welcome sight, the white night light, And the fly flew into the fire.

A gambler's yearn takes the turn 'cause dealers never tire.
Past the point of no return, The mind stretched like a wire.

Drained in vain, loser's bane, Whispering town crier.
Winner's loss, devil's gain. Back into the fryer.

My oh my! Whiskey high, Ten dollars she requires. What the hell, nothing lost
To satisfy desires.

For a pretty smile he'd walk a mile If she were still for hire.
On the hook, she read his book, If he's anxious, he's a buyer.

All down hill, he takes the spill, Cotton mouth gets dryer.
Drinkin', whorin', gamblin', Nothing to admire.

Smoke spiraled high, sweet smelling thighs, Fatuous blind flyer.
Temptress pie, smiling eyes, White fire dancing higher.

Rosy lips, bulbous tits, Whiskey breathing buyer. Gamblin' fool, lost his cool
As the fly flew into the fire.

Jaak - Somewhere around Singapore, 1974

On Sunday morning, Sanjo Casagrande decided that he had enjoyed his stay at the ranch about as much as he could possibly stand. He ate another tasty breakfast with his three new best friends Sarah Reid, Carol Mulhaney, and Jack Redhouse, and then bade them all a fond farewell. He said that he would miss them, and all the fun they had, as he promised to keep in touch. Then, as they reciprocated with their requisite ripostes, he grabbed Sarah by her small waist, kissed her passionately on the lips one last time, and hopped into his red Ford pick-up truck for the drive north. He waved a heart-felt Hi-Ho Silver, as he turned right out of the driveway racing east down Red Top road toward the airport, and attempted to put the trouble in Topeka behind him.

As he rounded the corner at the *Wamego Municipal Airport*, and turned north toward Kansas State Road 24, he noticed that Jack's plane was no longer tied down on the ramp. Then he remembered that Jack had returned the plane to his hangar at *Forbes Field* the day before. He thought about the events over the past few days; the *Jack of Clubs*, the wild rides, and his two new best friends *Pernicious* (Carol), and *Enchanté* (Sarah), and how Jack was really connected.

As he drove, he began to reflect, as well as question what had just happened. It had been a delightful diversion, but something just didn't feel right. Where did Jack learn to fly like that, and what was he really up to? How was Frank Valero tied in? Who were the two 'foreign suits' standing at the bar talking to Jack on Wednesday night? How did they fit in and what was their role? What was the big picture? What were his true feelings for Sarah Reid?

Vibrations from the road began to filter through the floorboard, increasing in frequency, as he began to make more connections. Not with just Jack, Carol, and Sarah, but with everybody and everything. There was much more to this make believe movie than was immediately apparent. There was the thing about the Topeka legislature and House Bill 2107 called the *Community Defense Act,* there were judges, lawyers, politicians, banks, community organizers, cops, bikers, wise guys, hookers, middlemen, money, private foreign accounts, covert operations, and links to organized crime. They were all connected, and it was everyone and everywhere. It was moral depravity, moral hazard, regressive behavior, a willingness to go along, apathy and complacency, and much more, all rolled into one. He could feel it. But how was he involved?

Nothing is real, It's just what we make it. We're making the motions, while we really just fake it" he thought to himself. Was his own reality something that was contrived, and he just chose to believe it as fact? Was it that he was taught various doctrines, that others believed to be reality, and therefore those beliefs became his reality? Was Sanjo really Jack? Maybe he was just reading too much into it. So he thought, and he questioned, and he resolved to find answers to his questions. Today, he thought that many things were again upside-down.

A Place to Call Home, Philippines

La Maison, Philippines, 1975

THE CASSANDRA CONUNDRUM

A man's work is nothing but this slow trek to rediscover,
through the detours of art, those two or three great and
simple images in whose presence his heart first opened.
- Albert Camus

The ominous April sky greeted Sanjo as he picked up Kansas State Road 24 and turned east. A towering wall of clouds separated the darkness to the west, from the sunshine to the east. A small spin-up twister twirled ahead of the approaching front. He made a left turn on highway 63 in the town of St. Mary's leading north past St. Mary's Airpark and Holy Cross road, then turned right heading east at Saxon road. When he reached Kansas State road 75 near Mayetta, he turned north again. The clouds to the west began to overtake his path, as he continued north on state road 75 for about forty miles, then turned right on 36 toward the I- 35 expressway that would take him up to Des Moines. Thunder rolled across the Kansas hills, and lightning pierced the dark quiet air as he began to reconstruct events of the past week that were vanishing in his rearview mirror. The swinging crucifix dangled beneath the mirror as he drove. "Wait a minute!" he said aloud, "If nothing is real, and it's just what we make it, then maybe the past week didn't really happen," he speculated.

Sanjo felt puzzled as reality began to set in. He had just spent the better part of a week living a fantasy, and was now heading home to Marissa. He enjoyed the flight, but wanted to avoid a hard landing. His mind rolled back to the days at the *California Club* in Olongapo when they were both young, and she was a dancer in the club. It seemed like yesterday, and in his mind, it virtually was. He needed some time to think. As he drove toward Des Moines, he dialed the 800-number for Hampton Inn reservations, and booked a room for the next two nights to prepare for his meeting on Tuesday.

With that done, he continued to drive as he sought answers to some niggling questions. The more he searched, the more he remembered that it wasn't a good idea to look for inner-deeper-hidden-meanings about life. Instead, he watched the mutating sky, and absorbed the blameless vibrations as he began to focus on the fact that he was driving along the surface of the Earth, a spinning planet that was being hurled around the sun at a speed of approximately 67,000 MPH. At that velocity, life was bound to get a little bumpy at times. In that light, his problems seemed less perplexing. It was at that moment that his cell phone rang. He didn't recognize the number on the display, but he pushed the green button anyway and said "Hello?'

"Hello, Sanjo, this is Sarah. How's the ride going?" she asked.

"Oh, Hi Sarah, just fine, thanks. I'm on I-35 about half way to Des Moines.

This is a surprise! What's up?" he responded anxiously.

"Well, I just wanted to see how you were doing. We didn't have very long to say goodbye, so I thought I would just call to tell you that Carol and I are beginning to miss you already" she said. "When will we see you again?" She asked.

"Well I miss you too Sarah, I had a good time in Topeka. In fact, it's been quite a while since I've had that much fun" he said. "But, I'm not sure. It's been over twenty years since I visited Jack the last time. I hope to keep in better touch this time around".

"Well, that's too long for me Sanjo, maybe it would be better if I just came up there to visit you in Duluth sometime in the next couple of months", she said with a laugh.

"Hmmm, that's probably not a good idea", he said. "I'm not sure that Marissa would be very understanding about another woman in my life at the moment".

"Besides, what about your work? What would Jack say?"

"In my line of work, there are lots of job opportunities" she said. "I can pretty much work wherever and whenever I choose. Besides, Jack doesn't mind. He can always find other girls to work in the club".

"I suppose that's true." said Sanjo.

"Well, let's just put that idea on the back burner for now. I'll see how things work out with my work schedule when I get back home, and we can talk again over the next few weeks. You have my cell number in any case, so you always know where to reach me," he said.

"Sure, Sanjo, OK. Well, I hope to hear from you soon. Otherwise, I may be tempted to hop on that Greyhound headed for Duluth". She insisted.

"Ha-ha" he chuckled. "Well, Sarah, there's no need for that. I'm sure that there are other gents in Topeka that can keep you company until we can hook up again. After all, it's not your first rodeo either. You can't be missing me that bad."

"That's true, Sanjo. But I think we make a pretty good team, and there are other team sports that the four of us may be able to get into" she said.

"Uh huh! I'm trying to picture that Sarah. What did you have in mind?

"Well for now, I'll just leave that to your imagination. The thing is that Jack, Carol, and I have a couple of other gigs going, that we would like to talk with you about some time. Based on our conversations, we think that you might be interested. Jack says that you're a stand-up guy, and that you're always looking for new adventures."

"Well, I like to keep busy, if that's what he means. But I'd have to hear more details before committing to anything. I need to watch my backside".

"We like watching your backside too Sanjo. So, I think that could work". "Haha. OK Sarah. So, we can talk more in the weeks ahead. You've piqued my interest."

With that, they said their goodbyes, promised to talk again soon, and ended the call. But Sanjo was beginning to feel that he needed some space. It was April, so he began to think about his annual Canadian fishing trip. He felt like he needed to be alone to have some time to think. And, what better place for some peace and serenity, than sitting in a boat in the middle of a remote Canadian lake, when fishing season opened? He could rent a little cabin with a boat on an island, relax, and eat fresh walleye while sorting things out in his mind. Then, he chuckled again at the thought of inviting Jack, Carol, and Sarah up to Canada with him on a "Walleye Hunting" expedition. And, what about Frank Valero? He might also enjoy the diversion as well. Of course, that would nullify the act of being alone. Although, in reality, it might be fun to go fishing with the four of them, he decided. He began to imagine *Enchanté* giving him a lap dance wearing only her cowgirl boots in the main room of the cabin, mingled with images of wooden boats, Red-Eye fishing lures, the cabin, Molsen Golden's, freshly caught walleye, and the girls dancing in the moonlight overlooking the lake, with the Northern Lights dancing in the backlit sky. "One could have their fish, and eat them too!" he thought.

Moments later, Sanjo's cell phone rang again; only this time it was Marissa. "Hello?" he answered again, surprised. Somehow, she knew that he had been talking to Sarah, he thought. Women are telepathic. "Hi Sanjo, are you headed home yet? she asked.

"Oh, hi Marissa. Actually, I am. I'm on I-35 about half way to Des Moines.

What's up?" he responded.

"Well, I haven't heard from you in a while, and I figured that you were probably on your way home, so I'm just calling to see how you're doing. How was your visit with Jack?"

"Well it was good to see him" he said. "He has quite the fabulous ranch, and he's doing very well. We had a nice time, but it also feels good to be heading home. He was probably glad to see me go as well. You know what they say, "it's nice to see friends come, … and it's also nice to see them go". As Sanjo ended the call, he promised to call her again when he checked into his hotel for the evening, and told her that he loved her. She was happy to hear him say the words. As he reflected on the call, he began to feel like he was being 'restricted to the ship', as he recalled another of Jack's poem's from years ago.

Scatterball-Dodgeball

New friends come, And old friends go,
But I just stay, and watch the show.

Some are strangers, Some I know,
Some are fast, and some are slow.

Some stay long, others can't wait.
The current swirls in the river of fate.

A point in time, A plot in space,
Another name, another face.

They move around me, With style and grace.
They move together, then lose their place. The river moves,
around the rock.
The shepherd stands, amid the flock.

Who are these people, In my life?
I watch their pain, I watch their strife.

They come and go, They never last.
But soon, I too will come to pass.

So, it seems
we're all the same.
Who made up this crazy game?

Jaak - Steaming around the Philippine islands, 1974

Perhaps a fishing trip with Jack, Frank, and the girls wouldn't be a bad idea, he thought. It had also been many years since he had last seen Frank, and a reunion might be good for all of them. Sanjo wondered again what the connection was with Frank, and how he came to be involved. Of course, Frank was always good with money, so it made sense that Jack would have called his old loan shark buddy to request some quick cash. It also made sense that Frank would be looking for new ways to invest his money. So, a fishing trip might help Sanjo to put the pieces of the puzzle together during a welcome break. When was the last time that he had seen Frank, he tried to recall. He thought that it might have been at the *California Club*, … but he couldn't quite remember that far back. Sanjo had slept a lot of nights since then.

Frank Valero left the ship in Subic Bay, and was discharged from the Navy many months before either Dick Redhouse or Sanjo Casagrande were released. On the morning that Frank departed, he had bumped into Redhouse in the town of Olongapo prior to taking a *Victory Liner* bus to Clark Air Base for his return flight home. Redhouse handed him a crumpled sheet of paper with a poem that he had scribbled earlier in the day, after spending the night with *Cassandra* at her little mud casa in the village. Redhouse had entitled the poem "*Olongapo*", and Frank had always appreciated that poem. What Dick Redhouse didn't know at the time, was that Frank had also spent a few pleasant nights with *Cassandra* when he was in port. In fact, it was Frank Valero that had introduced her to both Redhouse and Sanjo Casagrande during one of their jaunts at the *California Club* together. So, unbeknownst to the others, *Cassandra* had enjoyed the company of all three of them from time to time, but on separate occasions. Such was the nature of her work.

One curious characteristic about life aboard ship was that they all stood watches at their respective stations at different times. Not everyone was qualified for every watch. Watches stood 'in port' tended to be four hours on, and twelve hours off; or four on, and sixteen off, depending on resources in a particular division. Watches underway tended to be four on, and eight off. The watches were in addition to the normal workday from about 6:00 AM to 4:00 PM every weekday. At times, they could get one of their sailor buddies to stand their watch, in exchange for standing the other sailor's watch at a more convenient time. The point being that, not everyone could get liberty every night while in port. If they drew one of the evening watches, they might decide to remain aboard the ship that night and plan for liberty on the following night if it allowed them more time "on the beach". There was also the matter of pay. There was generally a limited amount of money available for buying drinks and women. Therefore, it wasn't good policy to spend all of one's money the first few days in port, and be without money until the following payday. Nevertheless, it was a common occurrence; so guys like Frank Valero made quite a lot of money operating "slush funds". That is, when someone would blow all of their money early, and were strapped for cash, they could always depend on guys like Frank to lend them $20 for $40; or $40 for $80. Meaning that, Frank would lend them $20 dollars when they needed it, if he was repaid on the following payday for $40. In that way, guys like Frank often had money to spare with their loan shark business, as well as more money in port to party. It was a smart way to operate. In fact when Frank got out of the Navy he used his slush fund money to buy a new Harley Davidson motorcycle to return to the 'Big Easy' city of New Orleans.

After he was discharged, Frank Valero returned home and was lucky enough to land a job working at a large shipyard in New Orleans, building US Navy and commercial ships. He also bought a new green Jeep CJ5 with a beige ragtop using his slush fund money as planned. The shipyards liked hiring ex-Navy guys like Frank because they knew their way around ships and equipment, and they knew how to weld on ships. In fact, it wasn't much of a transition at all. It was much like being back in the Navy because many of the guys that worked in the yards had the same background as Frank. So, the stories continued, and the work continued, and life rolled along from day to day. When his buddies Dick Redhouse and Sanjo Casagrande were released from active duty, they contacted Frank as they made the switch from military to civilian life; which nevertheless felt different. For example, they no longer had to stand watches every day, and there wasn't someone with a higher rank always telling them what to do. They could also rely on Frank to lend them some quick cash if needed while they found their footing. They discovered that they could easily think for themselves, and eventually adapted, although, they never quite lost the urge to paint an item that wasn't moving.

In any case, although life began to flow more smoothly for Frank, he was somewhat shocked when his little friend Yolanda from Olongapo showed up at the airport in New Orleans with her wedding dress about six months after he was discharged. He had, after all, promised to marry her when they were in the Philippines, and many of his sailor buddies had heard Frank declare that fact in the *California Club* during his last days in that party port. Apparently, he had forgotten about that little detail after he returned to the states. As it happened, New Orleans offered Frank more opportunities than he had anticipated, and as such, after a few weeks of frolicking around the 'Big Easy', Frank purchased a plane ticket for Yolanda's return trip home, after a rather long conversation about their misunderstanding. Frank also kept the Jeep CJ5 however, and still had it to the present day.

The three friends, Sanjo, Jack, and Frank kept in touch through Christmas cards once a year, and Frank, for lack of other news, would often write *"you can't make footprints in the sands of time, while sitting on your ass!"* in an effort to prompt Redhouse to publish his poems as promised. Then one day, long after dozens of Christmas cards had been exchanged, Redhouse called Frank with a proposition knowing that Frank was good with money, and could be trusted. That's when Frank Valero learned that Dick Redhouse's new name was now 'Jack', and they began to work on business ventures together. Frank was impressed with the way that Jack had pulled his life together, but could see no real advantage in telling him about his early relationship with *Cassandra*. So, it was still a veiled secret that the three of them had more in common than they thought.

FROM DARK TO LIGHT

My world was changing. It was early 1975 (or maybe late 1974), and I was getting short. About a year earlier, our sister ship, the 'Shasta', another *Kilauea-* class ammunition ship of the 7th Fleet, pulled into the berthing spot next to ours at the Naval Weapons Station in Concord, California. This was significant to me because one of the guys that was involved in the car crash with me in northern California over a year earlier, the driver actually, was a crewmember on the Shasta. I wanted to better understand the events following the crash, and the events that transpired after we left the transit barracks in TI for our ship assignments in WESPAC.

I departed the Flint and walked down the pier to where the Shasta was berthed, then climbed the accommodation ladder to their quarterdeck and requested 'permission to come aboard'. I asked the officer of the deck to contact my old transit buddy who was surprisingly still onboard. He came up to the quarterdeck and met with me, and it was a pleasure to see him again. We recounted the events of that fateful day, and as it happens, he hadn't gotten out of Dodge as quickly as I had, and was stuck in California after I left for the Philippines to face the consequences of the crash. Apparently, the car rental insurance hadn't covered the full collision cost of the rented vehicle, and my two transit buddies at the time got stuck with significant extra expenses for the wrecked car. In some ways, I was empathetic; except for the fact that I was the only one physically injured, and I hadn't crashed the car. I had been the passenger on that unfortunate day, and then was immediately sent overseas after the crash, with possibly a fractured neck. To this day, I'm not sure who paid for the hospital visit at the plastic surgeon's office.

While in the South China Seas, the ship would send our helo's over to Saigon daily to pick up the mail and bring it back to the ship. My mother had sent me a letter a couple of months into our cruise, while steaming around the coast of Vietnam, where she stated that she had recently received two peculiar pieces of mail. One of the items she received was a bill for a skull x-ray from a doctor in Northern California, and the other item was a front license plate from a car that I had crashed through a fence in Norman, Oklahoma while attending the Air Traffic Control school there. I sent a letter back to her requesting that she send the bill for the skull X-ray to the US Navy, and just throw the old license plate in the trash. We didn't have e-mail in those days (also no computers, no calculators, and no cell phones), so every message was sent by snail mail. I assume that the insurance covered the cost of the doctor's visit, or maybe the bill was sent to the Navy.

In any case, my buddy (let's just call him Sanjo for short) said that he didn't expect any sympathy from my end, and he was just glad that I had survived the crash. In fact, Sanjo admitted that he shouldn't have been behind the wheel that morning anyway, because he really didn't know how to drive. Sanjo said that he had wanted to learn from me. He said that he thought I was dead, and he prayed to Jesus to save my life; and after 10 minutes of beating on my chest on that grassy knoll in the middle of nowhere in northern California, I had let out a gasp of air (it seems to me that I was probably gasping for breath instead), sat up on the grassy knoll, looked around and asked "who am I?" "Where are we?", and "what are we doing here?" He said that he turned to religion after that day, because after he pulled me from the wreck, he promised Jesus that if I survived, he would give his life over to God. That was good to hear. He was just glad to see me after what we had both experienced over the past many months, and pleased that I was standing there with him on the quarterdeck on that bright sunny day. The 'Shasta' had visited many of the same WESPAC ports that were frequented by the 'Flint', but often at different times, according to different rotations, and changing circumstances. Both ships just happened to be in our 'home port', of Concord, California on this occasion, as fate would have it. Sanjo had met the 'love of his life' in the Philippines, and like a lot of other sailors I knew, was planning to bring her back to the 'States' some day. What could I say? I wasn't going to get in the middle of that decision. I was just glad that he was happy, and getting on with his life. Again, it wasn't "just a job, but an adventure". We said our goodbyes, and I thanked Sanjo once again for pulling me from the wreck on that magnificent morning in the Spring of 1973. We parted ways until some future day, when perhaps by chance, we might meet again.

But I digress. In the Spring of 1975 after refurbishment in San Francisco and some refresher training in San Diego, we were about to embark on another WESPAC cruise back to the South China Sea. The war was winding down, but we didn't know that. I reminded my chief about the deal I had made with the US Navy when I signed up in their DPPO program that stated I would serve two and a half years active duty, then return to civilian life and head back to college on the GI bill. They didn't want to hear it. By now, many of my 'steaming buddies' had been discharged and had returned to Wyoming, South Dakota, Washington, Minnesota, Michigan, Indiana, Ohio, Pennsylvania, Nebraska, New Mexico, Oklahoma, Arkansas, Louisiana, Kansas, East Texas, and many other origins in the heart of the country, North, South, East, and West, after a four or six year hitch. Actually, there were dozens (probably hundreds) of guys that just stayed in California near Concord, and married their Filipino and Asian girlfriends from the strip clubs and other venues of Olongapo, Kaohsiung, Sattahip, and Yokosuka, that they had met during their active duty days. We would often run into some of them in the local bars around the San Francisco Bay area after they had been discharged, and they told us of their exploits. But according to 'the powers that be' I was a 'critical rate' that they insisted needed to be on board for the next cruise. I was trying to angle for an early out, so they promised to take a look at my papers later. They also reminded me that I had actually signed up for six years in the Naval Reserves, which had me rather concerned. Were they not going to honor their end of the bargain? They promoted me to Petty Officer 2nd class, but I wasn't buying it. They wanted me in, and I wanted out. We agreed to disagree, and insisted that I ride the ship back to Subic Bay, Philippines. I wasn't a happy camper about that, but of course, I followed orders.

Our first stop was in Hawaii where we took on stores and ammo, as well as a supply of oil and jet fuel for whatever mission was planned. I believe that we spent almost a week in Pearl Harbor on that last trip. 'Pearl' was a pretty routine port of call for us since it was about the closest island available heading towards Southeast Asia after departing Concord. Still,

Pearl Harbor is located about 2000 nautical miles west of San Francisco, so steaming at an average of 15 knots/hour, it still took us a good six days to get there steaming 24 hours a day. Again, we were berthed a long way from any civilization at some distant pier in the middle of nowhere, and we would have to take a bus from Pearl Harbor to go into Honolulu for liberty. I know this quite well since I was one of the few bus drivers on board that had a commercial driver's license to take the liberty parties back and forth to town. I actually enjoyed this because it took me away from the ship, and took the place of my normal watch-standing duties aboard the Flint, which tended to be rather boring and mundane while in port. We didn't get much detailed information other than we were headed back to Subic Bay on our next stop. They used to say "if you don't hear a rumor every 15 minutes, start one". So we were getting information along with disinformation and weren't actually very sure about our next mission. Of course, we felt pretty good about going to the Philippines, but that decision could turn on a dime, and we could instead end up in Taiwan, Thailand, Japan, or elsewhere if command parameters changed.

I had been a pretty good sport up until that time, but these guys were beginning to 'grind my beans'. They knew the scoop, and they acknowledged that I had put in my time as agreed, and should receive new orders to rotate back to TI and get processed out. Nevertheless, they didn't relent. So one day, after busting up a couple of fights in Olongapo, while standing shore patrol duty, my dress whites got pretty grungy. I decided that the way to fix that was to take my dress whites into town to have them cleaned for the next Captain's inspection. The only thing that I didn't reveal to them was that I had planned to stay in Olongapo on unauthorized absence (UA), while the inspection occurred. I thought this might change their thinking about what a good soldier I was. Pretty stupid actually; because when I returned to the ship they confiscated my military ID, wrote me up, and restricted me to the ship, while they scheduled my own 'up close and personal' meeting with the Captain at the next 'Captain's Mast'. This is where they take all the bad apples to a 'Kangaroo Court' in front of the Captain, and typically fine them, bust them, and restrict them to the ship for getting out of line. Fortunately, I had been on fairly good terms with the Captain up until this little infraction, as I would often take pictures of my shipmates with the Captain, at his request, when one of them decided to 'ship over' (reenlist) for another four-year hitch. I think they thought that I might be doing the same thing; That is, 'shipping over'. Or, at least they may have desired that result. Nevertheless, I had different plans. So when they brought me in front of the Captain and read the charges against me, 'that I had gone UA, and missed the Captain's inspection' the Captain looked at me with a jaundiced eye and said something like "Tallinn, you know that you can't do this on the outside". Of course, the Captain knew that I was scheduled to be discharged, that we had a signed contract, that I wasn't about to ship over, and that all I really wanted was get new orders, head back to TI, get out of the Navy, and go back to college. I had learned enough about being a sailor by that time, and just wanted to be a civilian again. He knew that. The chiefs and ensigns standing around watching this little spectacle just wanted to see me get burned. So when it was my turn to respond I simply spoke the truth, and replied, 'Captain, if you'll just look the other way on this little misunderstanding, I'll hit the beach, get drunk on my ass, come back to the ship, pack my bag, and you'll never see me again.' So, you could have heard a pin drop when the Captain agreed, and just said 'Jaak, go on, … get out of here'.

Captain's Inspection, USS Flint (AE-32)

Lifer

I've been floatin' around in here for years It's the only place I know,
I'm down so low, that I'm in tears But there's no place left to go.

I used to be somebody else I was once a happy man,
But I've been here for so damn long I forgot just who I am.

Every day I get up slow Each day looks the same,
I never been this got-damn low I think I'm half insane.

Some have called it limbo, That seems to fit the bill,
The only place I've ever found Where time is standin' still.

They say some day that I'll get out That day seems far away,
The only thing that keeps me up I'm shorter every day.

Sometimes I feel happy,
But most the time I'm pissed,
But when my day comes to get out I'll probably re-enlist.

Jaak - US Navy, South Pacific, 1974

Of course, being true to my word, that's exactly what I did. I retrieved my military ID, picked up my new orders in the ship's office (that were already signed), and 'hit the beach' back into Olongapo. After exiting the main gate, I skipped into town (feeling quite a bit lighter on my feet), looked up one of my favorite girls in the California Club, and enjoyed my last night on the town in that stinky little party port. When I heard the roosters crowing the next morning, I made a beeline for the ship before the rest of the crew was up, packed my sea bag, and headed up to the quarterdeck. There, I requested permission to go ashore, showed my new orders to the officer of the deck, and headed for the bus. It was a magnificent morning, as I recall. Hot as hell though, as I made my way with my sea bag to the bus. But it didn't matter, I was headed to Clark Air Base in Manila, and nothing was going to get in my way, ... I thought.

Nevertheless, one must always be ready to improvise in the military. About half way through our little trek to Clark with a dozen other sailors, the bus broke down in the middle of the jungle with two flat tires (true story). Not to be discouraged, I got out of the bus stood alongside the two flat tires and stuck out my thumb. Two Filipino guys in an old beater of a car with no windows stopped and offered me a ride. A few other sailors were planning to go with me until they took a look at the Filipinos, then headed back to the busted down bus. Again, this didn't really concern me. As far as I was concerned, I was 'outta there'. So, I hopped into the car with the Filipinos and off we drove. They only spoke Tagalog, but I understood their language as they offered me a cold San Miguel beer from their six-pack, and away we went. Later, I found myself in a little jungle village in the middle of nowhere, in my now filthy dress whites, looking for another ride to Clark Air Base. A bus with all open air windows and clucking chickens took me to a nearby town where I was fortunate enough to catch a 'Victory Liner' bus back to Clark to beat the other bus.

There must be a benevolent power in the universe that watches over guys like me, otherwise my star would have burned out long ago. As it happens, I beat the bus with the other sailors that had broken down half way to Clark, by two hours, while they waited in the jungle heat for a new bus. I boarded a commercial jet bound for San Francisco, dressed in my mud spattered dress whites, and was again lucky enough to be sitting next to a gorgeous young Chinese gal who entertained me all the way back to California. It was her first trip to the States where she was planning to go to school. She had never met a 'real American sailor' before. We exchanged contact information prior to exiting the flight in California. A few months later a local newspaper interviewed her, and she told them about the nice sailor that she had met on her first flight to the United States. She sent me the article.

Before getting underway on the last cruise, I had bought a clean little green 1957 MGA coupe from a college professor in California for $350 bucks. I had spent several months pulling the engine and rebuilding the whole car at the base automotive shop at the Naval Weapons Station in Concord. So after I was processed out of TI, I spent another couple of weeks with a couple of girls that I knew near Walnut Creek, Brenda and Carmen, who were gracious enough to let me stay at their place while I made the final repairs to the MGA coupe, prior to heading back to the Midwest. If you recall, I had sold my '59 corvette prior to entering the Navy, so I needed another car for the return trip home.

The only part that I failed to replace was a 3-way bronze 'T' for the heater core. This turned out to be a mistake as I headed up the Colorado Rockies on my way to Wyoming on the return trip. By the time I reached Denver, my washrag sitting in my toilet kit on the back window ledge behind my seat was frozen solid, and so was I. So, I stopped by to visit another one of my old steaming buddies in Wyoming, who had been an Engineman with me in 'A-Gang' on the Flint. He let me stay at his place for a few days while I thawed out, and we were able to fabricate a new part for the heater core, which we also installed in the MGA. After that, I was 'home free' with 70°F cabin heat, and a much warmer ride back to Minneapolis to visit my cousins; then following that, back to Detroit.

Back in Detroit, I sent my application for admission to Engineering school and spent the next three years finishing up my college education on the GI Bill, graduating in August of 1978 with a Bachelor of Science Engineering, Mechanical, and received my 'Honorable Discharge' from the US Naval Reserves that same month.

Upon graduation, and after a couple of initial engineering jobs to get my feet wet, as well as a year spent recruiting engineers for a placement firm, I landed a 'Project Engineering' position in Milwaukee designing heat exchangers, and developing desalination plants for US Navy and commercial ships on projects for many of the well known shipbuilders in the country at that point in time. Working on a contract with NAVSEA (Naval Sea Systems Command) out of Bethesda, Maryland, one of my projects was to develop the first 'Mil-spec' Reverse Osmosis Desalination plant for US Navy Combatant ships. This meant that after it was built, it went through rigorous testing per Mil-Std 167, and Mil- S-901C Heavyweight Shock testing, as well as EMP testing, a six month seawater desalination test in Wrightsville Beach, North Carolina, and other tests as well as writing the tech manuals, maintenance procedures, and other related tasks. This was a four-year program. Upon completion of the tests, they cut a hole in the hull of a Destroyer (DDG Class) in Norfolk, Virginia, installed the RO Unit in the engine room aboard the ship, and I rode the ship to Puerto Rico with the crew to prove the concept. It worked so well that the Captain wouldn't let the Navy remove the unit from the engine room when the endurance test was completed. It was making all of their fresh water.

Concurrently, I was working on my MBA at a small local college in Milwaukee and graduated with my 'Master of Business Administration' degree in 1988, then went on to start my own Business Development Consulting business. The rest is history. Or as 'Winnie the Pooh' might say "Yesterday's history, tomorrow's a mystery, today is the present, that's why they call it a gift". I learned decades later from reading a 'Wikipedia' history of the USS Flint, that after I left the ship in Subic Bay, Philippines in the spring of 1975, that the 'Flint' went on to participate in 'Operation Frequent Wind' during the fall of Saigon at the end of the Vietnam war. I missed that one, as I was driving my green '57 MGA coupe back to Detroit from San Francisco at about that time, happily double-clutching every shift, as I made my way back to the Midwest. In later years, the 'Flint' was transferred to the Military Sealift Command and the two groups of twin mount 3"/50 caliber guns, and 'Phalanx' close-in weapon systems (CIWS) were removed from their mounts, as they installed a civilian crew to support this type of support mission.

And that, as Paul Harvey might say, 'is the rest of the story'.

In retrospect, I believe that the 'Fall of Saigon' in the Spring of 1975, actually demonstrated the impotence of big government control over sovereign nations. It also illustrated the senseless waste, huge costs, and empty depravity of such a vacuous exercise as war by big governments, instigated under questionable circumstances. In other words, 'what the hell were we doing there to begin with'? Perhaps it was all just about finding new sources of oil.

In fact, General Smedley Butler was most likely correct when he stated that "War is a Racket". https://en.wikipedia.org/wiki/War_Is_a_Racket

As it happens, perhaps because I'm older now, and because hindsight tends to be 20/20, it often seems to me that the 'military' is a mere tool used by big government to influence geo-political and macroeconomic events, as well as effect control over sovereign nations for the exploitation of their resources. More and more, as I see the term 'elites' written in the mainstream press, I substitute the word 'elite', with the word 'Satan'; Primarily because I believe that this may be the entity that actually

116

pulls the levers in these events. It's my belief that no entity, or group of individuals should have 'carte blanche' control over other individuals in the normal course of events. And, perhaps the 'Althing' model of government is a better example to follow for all people that actually desire to form a government 'of the people', and 'for the people'. Everything else seems to be just more noise. https://en.wikipedia.org/wiki/Althing

In the end, the only real power in the world that can have a lasting effect for peace, respectability, and survival of the world, is the power of Love. Everything else is secondary, and that is demonstrated every day in our individual worlds, within our own families, and within our circle of friends.

So, maybe I hit my head pretty hard on that remarkable sunny morning in the Spring of 1973 as we smashed into the telephone pole with a rental car heading south down the California coast. And perhaps, the transition from dark to light happened in that instant, as I gasped for a breath of fresh northern California air, sitting there with Sanjo on that grassy knoll, with my head, face, and hair full of shattered glass, wondering who I was, where I was, and why we were there, … with the acknowledgement that, … at that very moment, … nothing was real, … and much of what we've been taught, is primarily bullshit!

Real-eyes

Nothing is real;
It's just what we make it.
We're making the motions
While we really just fake it.

They feed us the data,
and like fools we take it'.
Trying to expand our mind;
Instead we just bake it.

When will it end,
This, follow the leader?

Jaak - Spring of 1973, on a grassy knoll in northern California

My 1957 MGA California Cross-Country Coupe

CAYMAN CAPERS, AND PANAMA PAPERS

Sanjo arrived at the Hampton Inn in Des Moines on Sunday evening after another long drive. He spent some quiet time in his hotel room soothing his soul. He felt exhausted from the trip and his many troubling ruminations. Since his meeting was scheduled for Tuesday, he had more time to work through his presentation. He felt somewhat burdened with thoughts about work, as well as his home life. Not that there were many heavy burdens that he faced; only that, well, he had a lot on his mind. He liked mulling over the small details in his head to ward off problems. Nonetheless, he felt like he was approaching a red line. Or, perhaps it was a 'Redhouse' line.

The more he pondered the fishing trip, the more he began to believe that it was a good idea. He would call Jack and the others to set it up. Something had to change, and a fishing trip might act as a catalyst to move his life forward. He felt that he might be entering some sort of mid-life crisis. He wasn't at all sure how he was going to arrange a fishing trip with "the boys", plus bring "the girls", but he would worry about that later. Now at the hotel, he remembered that he had promised to return Marissa's earlier call as he dialed his home number.

"Hi, it's me" said Sanjo when Marissa answered. "I'm settled in the hotel now, so it's easier to talk, than when I'm driving".

"Yes, I was just wondering about your plans. We haven't talked in a while". "Well, I think I need a vacation from my vacation. It was good to see Jack. I have a meeting planned for Tuesday, but since it's April, I was also thinking about my annual fishing trip in June".

"I think that I'm the one that needs a vacation", said Marissa. "You travel all the time. Maybe we could plan a trip together, where it's warm".

"That's true. It might be good for us" said Sanjo. "What did you have in mind?"

"Well, maybe Albuquerque for a few days. Just to relax in the sunshine and dry air".

"Sure, I can look at some of the travel websites to check flights and hotels. Maybe we can get some quick cheap flights with a hotel room included for a long weekend. Would that work?"

"Maybe. I think I just need a break from Duluth for a while. I could also use some warmer weather, and some quiet time with my busy husband."

Sanjo: "I see. Well, sure. Let me do some checking and see what I can find. If that works, would you mind if I planned a fishing trip with Jack, and maybe Frank Valero?"

Marissa: "Frank? When did he enter the picture?

Sanjo: "Well, it was just a thought. Jack and I were talking about the fishing trip, and thought Frank might be interested too. Jack and Frank have been working on a couple of projects together, so we thought that it might be good to also include Frank this time around."

Marissa: "Well, let's talk about it more when you get home. That surprises me a little".

Sanjo: "Sure, I understand. I've got a lot to think about anyway with this meeting coming up. So, yeah, let's talk about it more when I get home". He said. "I'm not really sure where I'm going with all of this anyway".

As Tuesday rolled around, Sanjo's meeting with the company in Des Moines with Randy Bidwell and the others went smoothly; and as usual, not much changed, but they all agreed to move the process forward. They agreed to increase grain sales by about 10% in the near future, along with a few ideas to help decrease the company's production costs, so Sanjo and everyone else in the meeting seemed satisfied with the results. They thanked Sanjo for being such a valuable and integral part of the team, and expressed gratitude for his input. Their little get-together lasted for about an hour and a half before it broke up and everyone went their separate ways. The meeting was actually a minor factor in a life that was beginning to get a bit more complicated. Sanjo had already checked out of his hotel on Tuesday morning, so as he left the meeting he pointed his pick-up truck north toward Duluth to begin the long journey home.

Back on the road, heading north towards Duluth, Sanjo called Jack to propose a Canadian fishing trip with himself and the girls to get that ball rolling. However, he was a bit surprised by Jack's response.

"Hey Jack, it's Sanjo. Have you recovered from our little get-together yet?" he asked.

"Haa-ha-ha. Hi Sanjo. You know me, I take everything in stride. Your little visit energized me, so I'm actually feeling pretty good. What's up?" asked Jack.

"Well, do you remember our little talk about a fishing trip in Canada?" "Yeah, sure. As I said, it sounds like a good time" Jack responded.

"Well, what do you think about setting up a little trip to Canada in June, with you, me, and maybe Frank, and the girls. I could make the arrangements if you're interested." suggested Sanjo.

"To tell you the truth Sanjo, although I'm sure it would be a good time, I'm not too big on the Canadian route myself", said Jack. "What would you think about a deep sea fishing trip instead? Like the trips we used to go on in the Philippines? I know Frank has got some good connections down in the Gulf, … but we might also consider going down to the Caribbean; Maybe to the Caymans, or the Dominican Republic, or off the coast of Cuba; or perhaps down to Panama in Central America. How does that sound?"

It seemed to Sanjo that Jack was already laying the groundwork for his next 'project', and knew that he couldn't "*make footprints in the sands of time, while sitting on his ass!*" Maybe it was time to hatch such a plan. Apparently, there were a lot of 'businessmen' in Kansas, who had reasons to just disappear, as well as find ways to 'shelter' their hard earned savings in various offshore accounts, and Jack's Russian buddies had some clever ideas on how to turn this market need into a profitable new business venture down in Panama.

Meanwhile, back in Duluth, Marissa too, was beginning to smell something 'fishy' going on with the 'boys'. And, knowing her husband Sanjo, Frank Valero, and 'Jack' Redhouse as well as she did from her previous intimate relationships with all three of them, decided that it was probably time to have a 'Come to Jesus' conversation with Sanjo when he landed back in Minnesota. Being the telepathic female that she was, she also sensed that more had happened down in Kansas than Sanjo was letting on, or as Dorothy in the 'Wizard of Oz' might say to her pup Toto, 'I have a feeling that we're not in Kansas anymore'. And that's exactly the way it happened when Sanjo returned home and began to get more religion. Feeling quite guilty, as well as chagrined about his recent spring fling with his buddy Jack, and the girls, *Pernicious*, and *Enchanté*, Sanjo decided to come clean with 'Cassandra' and tell her all that had happened (well most of it); which in the end, helped to strengthen their relationship at this juncture in their lives, as Cassandra learned how to lap dance again, and began to demonstrate to Sanjo that she still had what it takes, and was still the best dancer from the '*California Club*'.

In fact, they connected so well after their little 'Come to Jesus' discussion that Sanjo got back on the horn with Frank, Jack, Carol Mulhaney (aka; *Pernicious*) and Sarah Reid (aka; *Enchanté*), and informed them that the little fishing expedition would need to be postponed indefinitely, and that he actually didn't see many more business trips coming up in the near, or distant future that might carry him down that way again. Of course, Sarah was a bit disappointed to hear the news, but quickly rotated to Frank, and the game was on again for the four of them in Kansas, as they prepared their plans for Panama.

People began to panic when the Panama Papers peppered the news in the beginning of the year. The full report was said to be coming out in May of 2016, and there would be more questions than answers as details were revealed to the general public. Sanjo's instincts told him that Jack was probably planning something bigger than just a fishing trip, so, although he was intrigued, he was also beginning to get cold feet. What was Jack up to now, he wondered? Knowing Jack and Frank as he did, and their many money making schemes, he was a bit reluctant about getting mixed up in some new diabolical debacle this far along in his life. Things had worked out fairly well for Sanjo up until that point, and he felt that he was getting too old for this kind of crap anyway. He also decided that the best thing that ever happened to him in his life was Marissa Casagrande (Née, Marikit), (aka; "Cassandra") the mother of young Francis and his daughter, who was also a pretty damn good dancer herself, and who just also happened to be, Sanjo's wife.

So, in the end, Sanjo bowed out, while the other four (Jack, Frank, *Pernicious*, and *Enchanté*) pursued their plans to begin sheltering funds for their foreign friends in Panama, while filtering cash through the 'Jack of Clubs', then concealing the money in Panamanian accounts run by the many selected law firms headquartered in Panamanian ports. They believed that they weren't really doing anything illegal, as they just sent the extra funds to the lawyers in Panama that supervised most of the accounting work, and their function was merely to keep the funds rolling. This was fairly easy for Jack, Frank, *Pernicious*, and *Enchanté,* since most of their transactions were in cash sales anyway, and they merely needed to 'bundle it', exchange the money for bonds or T-bills, and/or carry the cash to Panama for processing. They took a respectable 8% commission for their troubles, which amounted to a good chunk of change for the four of them, and also covered their expenses, which they eventually used to establish their own offshore fund in a Panamanian offshore trust under the name 'Victory Liner Trust' with their proceeds.

From a business perspective, they rationalized that it was actually against the US Constitution to confiscate property from US citizens without permission in any case, and without adequate compensation. After all, one's labor is one's property. And it's against the fifth amendment to the US Constitution for the government to confiscate one's property.

http://constitution.findlaw.com/amendment5/annotation15.html

In business, Sales minus the Cost of Sales equals Profit. Profit (income) can be taxed, … but your labor (i.e., wages) should not be taxed. Your wages are part of the 'Cost of Sales'. Your wages are not income, they are your property, … thus should be included in the cost of sales, and not taxed as part of your income.

Consequently, they believed that all US 'income tax' on wages were illegal, and shouldn't be subject to confiscation in the first place. Only profit or 'income' should be taxed. That's why the government states that taxes are 'voluntary'. The government cannot legally confiscate your property. That's what happens when you sign your tax returns; you are actually volunteering to give a large portion of your wages (your property) to an international corporation (the IRS). The Federal Reserve (corporation) lends 'notes' to the US Treasury and they call it 'money', when actually it's just another form of debt. They think it's funny. The IRS then, is nothing more than the 'enforcement arm' of the Federal Reserve 'Corporation', another illegal entity according to a strict interpretation of the US Constitution. Pay the money, or they'll break your legs. Then, on the notes (debt) that they actually let you keep, you are taxed on every dollar that you spend. It begs the question, 'Is any of it legal, or is it all structured to support a criminal, corrupt, immoral, unethical, and illegal federal government pyramid scheme that's more inclined to start new wars (morally bankrupt) with the proceeds, than build infrastructure and support it's citizens'?

Furthermore, 'Income Taxes' have grown from 3%, from around the period just after the civil war, to virtually 50%, when one considers that much of the money that one is allowed to keep is also taxed again, when the money is spent on goods or services. Nice work if you can get it!

With the volume of extra cash that Jack, Frank, and the girls were hauling in for their 'clients', they were able to buy a nice little motor yacht that Frank found down on the Gulf Coast near New Orleans. It was actually an older US Navy Yard Patrol Craft (YP), with hull number 'YP-504', that they had refurbished at one of the local shipbuilders near Mobile, Alabama. They renamed the patrol boat 'Victory Liner' in honor of the bus company that operated between Subic Bay and Manila in the Philippines, and the four of them fondly referred to her as just 'Victory Liner 504'. They used their little motor yacht for their special getaways together as they plied their way to Panama and back. It had plenty of berthing space for all four of them, plus room for a few more, as well as a nice rear deck for late night parties where they would combine rum and coke with calypso music, and watch the romantic moon rise over the bewitching waters in the Gulf of Mexico as they scanned the night skies for the occasional UFO. It was a lot like being back in the Navy again they decided; only they were doing the work of both the captain and the crew as they traveled from party port, to party port, back and forth, up and down, all the way to Panama City and back with stops in Cancun, Belize City, and other ports along the way. And, they rarely ever had to stand another boring watch again.

Ultimately, Frank and Jack also invited Sanjo and Cassandra to join them on their island hopping far-flung forays in the Caribbean and the Gulf, as every one of them truly enjoyed Sanjo and Cassandra's company anyway, and remembered how well Cassandra could dance. They were all adults, and at this point in their lives realized that many relationships often became rather dysfunctional, or complicated, or conflicted, or confused in any case. They all enjoyed their little holidays together, and it gave Jack, Frank and Sanjo a chance to catch up, as well as do a little deep sea fishing for swordfish, tarpon, and tuna in the gulf, as they steamed merrily, merrily gently down the stream. Sanjo Casagrande, for his part, believed that the whole group had 'quantum jumped' to a new reality as they felt the strong love vibrations at 528 Hertz while cruising the countless coasts.

The only person that suffered a little heartbreak was Yolanda, Frank's wife, after Frank rotated to Sarah Reid (aka; *Enchanté*). In the end, Frank settled up with Yolanda so that she was fairly comfortable and content down in the 'Big Easy' when Frank retired from 'corporate' life. Nevertheless, the two of them agreed to let Frank keep his CJ5 jeep and Harley Davidson motorcycle that Frank had purchased with his slush funds upon leaving the Navy. Merrily, merrily, merrily, merrily, life was but a dream.

So, in the end, when viewed from their perspective, life was like a business. There was profit and loss, as well as plenty of risk. It required investment in time, resources, and assets to realize rewards. They all needed cash flow. More in, … and less out, to meet expenses, and payroll. They invested in themselves and others, as they grew. Yet, they constantly strived to know themselves better as they hoped and prayed that 'the saints would provide', and everything would work out to their benefit, … in their continued quest for their own independence. Still, in December of every year, the three friends, Sanjo, Jack, and Frank kept in touch through their annual Christmas cards. And, as was customary with Frank, who was reluctant to give away any confidential information, or disclose any personal or intimate details, would often just scribble a short note on the bottom of his card that read;

"You can't make footprints in the sands of time, … while sitting on your ass!"

Merry Christmas!

Riding the Water Buffaloes, Philippines, 1975

SELECTED POEMS

To help maintain my harmony and balance, I wrote poems and took pictures when I wasn't playing cards in a game of 'Spades'. Below are a few poems I wrote mostly during WESPAC cruises.

LOOSE ENDS
REAL-EYES
WATCHSTANDER
OLONGAPO
SCHOOL CALL
DOWN ON THE FARM
LIGHT WINGS
TEMPTRESS
SCATTEBALL-DODGEBALL
LIFER
NUTS
SHORT-TIMER
ONE MORNING, OVER EASY
CLEAR THE MESS DECKS
MAIL CALL
THE LIEUTENANT
NANAIMO
NICKELS & DIMES
SKATE
JUST ADJUST

Looose Ends

I want to be alone,
I mean really alone.
No family, no face,
no friends.

I want to be a stone,
a colorless stone,
no home, no ties,
loose ends!

I want to be free;
I mean really free!
No parties, no noise;
just quiet.
I want to be me, only lonely me.
I want to be free to try it.

I want to roam,
without a home,
to hike, or bike,
or thumb it.

To be a poem.
A lone Jerome.
I'd like to cleanly
bum it.

I want to blend,
and not pretend
to be something
I'm not.

I want to end,
and start again,
and see
just what I've got.

A colorless stone,
a buried bone,
an island, a cloud,
a sonnet.
On my own.
A pale tone.
a sail, airfoil,
or comet!

Jaak - 1973, South China Sea

128

Real-eyes

Nothing is real;
It's just what we make it.
We're making the motions
While we really just fake it.

They feed us the data,
and like fools we take it'.
Trying to expand our mind;
Instead we just bake it.

When will it end,
This follow the leader?

Jaak - South China Sea, 1973

Watchstander

The ocean was as ruffled silk,
The night air, clear and still.
The moon sat like a golf ball
on a darkened window sill.

Clouds sailed by before it,
Partly covering its face,
As I stared across the water
through the dimly lighted space.

Enveloped in morning mist,
I watched the morning moon.
The last hours of the watch,
And the Sun would be up soon.

The sky was looking brighter,
partly cloudy in the East.
The daylight was approaching,
the wind had almost ceased.

Below the surface of the water,
Underneath reflected sky,
I watched the morning twilight
as the star lights floated by.

Grey cotton clouds hung in the air,
Underneath the blue,
Orange horseshoe of horizon,
Complementary hue.

The blending of the morning
Overtakes the night.
It's show time every sunrise
With the ever-changing light.

The minutes passing faster
while my mind was at a rest,
on the last minutes of the watch
as I sat as mornings guest.

How happy is the watchstander
At quiet times like this.
"It's almost worth the hassle",
I said, in playful jest.

Jaak - Indian Ocean, 1973

Olongapo

I'm bunked down drunk,
And my stomach's in knots;
I got a P.I. honey, and the G.I. trots.
It's been eight long hours since I took the ride
From the shipboard boogie to the other side.

I feel hung over
With the roosters crowin'
Soundin' reveille loud as bugles blowin'.
I'd feel much better where there's no one round
To hear the beatin' 'tween my eardrums pound.
In a quiet little corner, where there's no more sound,
While my head's goin' through the lost and found.

The body next to me is brown,
But all I can manage is a gaseous frown,
'cause a high ain't nothin' when you're comin' down
from a night long cruise in a party town;
when all you got left is an empty head,
and your honey's got your money, and she looks half dead.
All you can do is hold your bed
And try to forget the things you've said.

But, if I had it all to do over again,
I'd do it all the same.
When there's no one round to tuck you in at night,
There's no one round to blame.

And, I'm gonna quit drinkin'
And give up my smoke
After one more drink,
And one more toke.
I'm serious now, that ain't no joke.
I must be half insane!

Jaak - Subic Bay, Olongapo, Philippines, 1973

School Call

I've been going to school a long time now,
It seems a sort of bind,
The school is called the school of life,
I've been taking one course at a time.

I started walking at sixteen months
They told me I was slow.
But I just do things my own way
The only way I know.

Once I knew a gambler,
His sleeves held many tricks.
But now his sleeves are empty,
And he's into politics.

If you haven't a million by twenty-five,
I'm told you never will.
Unless, of course, you pay your way
By dipping in the till.

I asked one man what I should do
To put me in the pink.
He told me in one simple word
That I should stop and THINK.

I once had many questions
'cause I used to think a lot.
But now I've heard the answers;
That's why I drink a lot.

I'm getting lost for answers
As to just what I must do,
To get ahead in this backward world
Before I bid adieu.

So, I'll just keep taking courses
'til I find something I like;
or wind up empty minded
like the rest of mankind's psych.

But what have I to lose at all?
Indeed! What have I to gain?
Just another school call!
To me, it's all the same!

Jaak - Concord, California, 1974

Down on the Farm

I didn't want to settle down,
It wasn't in my plan.
But now I don't know where to go,
Since I've hit fertile land.

She came upon me softly,
Sort of snuck up from behind.
We spent some time together,
Then she coyly blew my mind.

She said "I've a surprise for you,
I think you ought to hear!"
I think that I am pregnant.
How do you like that dear?"

I nearly lost my little head,
My mind went sort of blank.
My dreams sailed by before me,
My dreamboat passed and sank.

"What is your plan of action?"
I asked in plain remorse.
She looked at me in disbelief;
"To marry you, of course!"

I thought that I could leave her.
I started to regress.
But, I knew too well that she must have
My true name, and address.

I don't really want to marry her,
I don't know if I can.
But now I don't know where to go,
Since I've hit fertile land.

Jaak - Somewhere in the Pacific, 1974

Light Wings

White wings
Light wings
These are all the right things.
They are what are on my mind
I think about them most the time.

Tight wings,
Taut with canvas stretched.
Lighter than air
Very fair.

Floating over the runway
With the greatest care,
And then they flare.

Nothing else makes much sense
As I watch the plane's descent's
The joy I feel is immense
As I watch them fly.

Many trees are standing bare
In the breeze of the warm fall air
And I haven't a single care
As I watch them fly.

White wings
Light wings
These are all the right things
Kite strings
Bright things

Of them I am aware.

Jaak - Buchanan Field, Concord, California, 1974

Temptress

Curvaceous thighs, smoke spiraled highs,
Money hungry friars.
Cherry pie, ham on rye,
Sink into the mire.

A futile try, the devils' lie
Cried to take him higher.
A welcome sight, the white night light,
And the fly flew into the fire.

A gambler's yearn takes the turn
'cause dealers never tire.
Past the point of no return,
The mind stretched like a wire.

Drained in vain, loser's bane,
Whispering town crier.
Winner's loss, devil's gain.
Back into the fryer.

My oh my! Whiskey high,
Ten dollars she requires.
What the hell, nothing lost
To satisfy desires.

For a pretty smile he'd walk a mile
If she were still for hire.
On the hook, she read his book,
If he's anxious, he's a buyer.

All down hill, he takes the spill,
Cotton mouth gets dryer.
Drinkin', whorin', gamblin',
Nothing to admire.

Smoke spiraled high, sweet smelling thighs,
Fatuous blind flyer.
Temptress pie, smiling eyes,
White fire dancing higher.

Rosy lips, bulbous tits,
Whiskey breathing buyer.
Gamblin' fool, lost his cool
As the fly flew into the fire.

Jaak - South China Seas, 1974.

Scatterball-Dodgeball

New friends come,
And old friends go,
But I just stay, and watch the show.

Some are strangers,
Some I know,
Some are fast, and some are slow.

Some stay long,
others can't wait.
The current swirls in the river of fate.

A point in time,
A plot in space,
Another name, another face.

They move around me,
With style and grace.
They move together, then lose their place.

The river moves,
around the rock.
The shepherd stands, amid the flock.

Who are these people,
In my life?
I watch their pain, I watch their strife.

They come and go,
They never last.
But soon, I too will come to pass.

So, it seems
we're all the same.
Who made up this crazy game?

Jaak - South China Sea, 1973

Lifer

I've been floatin' around in here for years
It's the only place I know
I'm down so low, that I'm in tears
But there's no place left to go.

I used to be somebody else
I was once a happy man
But I've been here for so damn long
I forgot just who I am.

Every day I get up slow
Each day looks the same
I never been this got-damn low
I think I'm half insane.

Some have called it limbo;
That seems to fit the bill
The only place I've ever found
Where time is standin' still.

They say some day that I'll get out
That day seems far away
The only thing that keeps me up
I'm shorter every day.

Sometimes I feel happy
But most the time I'm pissed
But when my day comes to get out
I'll probably re-enlist.

Jaak - US Navy, South Pacific, 1974

Nuts

Old man sitting on a stone park bench
Underneath a sycamore tree.
The bench as old as the earth is new
But how old can a sycamore be?

Children play in the green grass park,
Their lives seem careless and free.
Squirrels squeal on the ground
While the children chirp in the trees.

Listening to the warm thin breeze,
It promises eternity.
But the old man knows in his crying heart
That life's gonna set him free.

Farewell foolish young childhood,
Empty dreams that seemed to flee.
The older you get, the wiser you are.
Old man was too late to see.

How sweet is sweet young innocence?
How bitter is reality?
How soon do you learn the bitter truth?
How sweet is your melancholy?

Dead leaves dance in an autumn breeze
Where a sycamore used to be.
And another seed grows
Next to a stone park bench
Where begins a new sycamore tree.

Jaak - South China Seas, 1974

Short-Timer

At Five years old
You wonder who, and why, and how, and when;
And at Ten,
You think how young you were
When you lived way back then.

At Fifteen you discover how much there is to learn;
And at Twenty, you piece together
All you've strived so hard to earn.
But at Twenty-five, you realize
There's nothing left to spend.

So, at Thirty, things start picking up
And you get your head together;
And at Thirty-five you're doing fine,
And things are looking better.
But at Forty years you ask yourself
"What is my life's work worth"?
and, by Forty-five you're questioning
the reason for your birth.
So, at Fifty you're reborn again
And become a real go-getter.

By Fifty-five, your world has changed
And things just aren't the same;
And at Sixty you're pretty tired of
Playing life's weary game.
At Sixty-five, you're amazed
At all the things gone wrong;
And at Seventy, you realize,

Your past has come and gone.
So at Seventy-five you sit and laugh
At all your long past pain.

But it all passes by so quickly that
It's gone before you know it;
And it takes less time to beat the clock,
Than it does to up and throw it!
So before you frown about the thought
That life is such a downer,
Picture your life the way you would
If you were an "out-of-towner".
'Cause it takes less time to spend a life,
Than it does to grow it;
And it won't be long.

Jaak - Somewhere in the Pacific, 1974

One Morning, Over Easy

The sky is green,
The sea deep blue,
The horizon, sort of yellow.

With my eggs half down
And the sun half up,
I'm feelin' pretty mellow.

With a well-earned yawn
I watch the dawn,
As the sun breaks the horizon.
The water shakes a shiver of warmth
As the sun continues risin'.

"Another new day is comin' my way",
I say, as it approaches;
Then kick the deck and turn around
To sweep up all the roaches.

A bland new day to waste away,
It isn't worth a quarter.
Just one more day
That I can say,
"I'm pleased I'm getting shorter!"

Jaak - 1974, Indian Ocean, Gulf of Aden

Clear The Mess Decks!

Stand in line for every meal;
Stand in line and sweat;
Lifers cut in front of me,
And this is what I get.

Fingerprints in my butter,
Cookie crumbs in my bread,
They just ran out of jelly,
And the peanut butter won't spread.

The hamburgers are soooo greasy,
All the French Fries too!
I gained ten pounds just yesterday,
It's more than I can chew.

I stand in line for breakfast
Just to get that scrambled egg.
Everybody's bitchin'
And the messcook's on the rag!

Stand in line at lunch time
Grab all that you can!
Throw away most all of it
So they don't serve it again!

Stand in line for dinner
Man, this sure is fun!
Eat like it's your last meal
Then grab your tray and run.

I stand in line for breakfast;
Stand in line for lunch;
Stand in line for dinner
With the finest of the bunch!

Perhaps I'll start a diet;
Maybe then I won't get stout.
I'll just start skipping every meal,
Maybe then they'll let me out!

Jaak - 1973, South China Seas

Mail Call

I wonder if she wrote to me?
I need to hear a tale.
Hurry up there mail PO,
Run and fetch the mail.

I wonder if she still loves me;
Maybe she's in jail.
I wonder what she's doing now;
I'd better get some mail.

Bring me back a letter;
I don't care if it's braile;
Bring me back a postcard;
But, bring me back some mail.

She said that she would write to me.
She said she wouldn't fail.
She hadn't better let me down;
Where's my blasted mail?

Bring me back some mail friend
Bring it in a pail;
Bring it in a wheelbarrow,
All my precious mail.

Bring back all my letters;
I want to hear a tale,
Here comes that damn mail PO, Hey!
Where's all my mail?

She said that she would write to me;
She said she wouldn't fail.
Hey there, little bar maid!
Bring me another ale!

Jaak - South China Seas, 1974

The Lieutenant

Hey, Fat Rat, where's your bone head at?
Why must you hassle me so?
You've got me going in circles,
And I can't seem to find a hole.

What is this maze you've trapped me in?
What is this maddening craze?
Why must you keep me guessing?
I can't see through the haze.

I'm not a little guinea pig
That you can put to test.
You must have me mistaken
For something you've possessed!

I'm not a new experiment
Later you will see.
Why must you try my patience
When I'm trying to break free?

Hey! Fat Rat!
I've you down pat.
Your folly can't last much longer.
I'm much too smart for this dull part,
You'll see that I'm much stronger.

I'll turn your little world around
And start a brand new page,
When I get out
And watch you run
Around your little cage.

Jaak - Somewhere in the Pacific, 1974

147

Nanaimo

The day was even nicer
The day I left the town.
But things were getting noisy
And I couldn't stick around.

Nanaimo was the city's name
The nicest that I've found.
But things were getting noisy
And I didn't like the sound.

When I first arrived in town,
The view was simply grand.
But after two short days there
I packed my bags and ran.

Down to the Greyhound station
I caught the south-bound stage.
Knowing when to leave, I say
Only comes with age.

And that's the way I saw it
Everybody was a clown.
The day I left Nanaimo
When the Shriners came to town.

Jaak - 1973 "Stand-down", after first WESPAC Cruise, back from Vietnam

Nickels & Dimes

I think I'll die,
I don't know why,
It doesn't make much sense.

Life's passed me by,
I watched her fly.
I haven't slept good since.

When I was young,
I used to think
That life was milk and honey.

But, that's no good,
Now that I'm old,
Without a stash of money.

How fast she went,
How fast I spent,
My life, and all my bread.

What will I do
Without a cent?
I'd be much better dead!

I think I'll die,
Why should I try
To make myself convince?

That I should stay,
And grope my way
Each little crummy inch.

Jaak - 1974, Somewhere in the Pacific

Skate

Who skates the most
Who rates the most
Who makes the greatest story?

Who tells me how,
Who tells me now,
Who has the greatest glory?

Who is this guy
Who tells me why,
And when, and where, How often?

And who am I
Who lets him lie,
Who makes my life less softened?

Who is that skate
I think I hate,
His rotten bones there walkin'.

Who is that Skate
How do he rate,
To whom's he think he's talkin'?

Why must I work
For that dumb jerk,
Who does he think he's foolin'?

What is this quirk?
I stand and perk,
While he just sits there droolin'

What is this fate
How do he rate,
What is this situation?

Guess I'll make rate
So I can skate,
And take my own vacation.

Jaak - 1973, South China Sea

150

Just Adjust

Some might say
We chose this place
Before the earth was dust.

And, some would say
'That's just not so';
The old ones rose through crust.

My brother said that we must do,
just what we think we must,
And therefore, should consider most,
the things that don't go bust.

He also said that life's a trust,
And, that his mind is toast;
And of all the things he ever lost,
His mind, he misses most.

Our thoughts get tossed
From to, through fro,
we ponder, and we fuss.
But after all is said and done,
They're adjusted, as discussed.

Transcending all dimensions
Through all things frivolous
In existential furor;
It's just ridiculous.

Dost thou live forever?
Or did we just get thrust
From somewhere long forgotten,
And tossed beneath the bus?

'It probably shouldn't matter,
Since most roads lead to thus;
The seven mountained city
with its frankincense and lust.

In constant contravention,
with manifest mistrust,
Consensus in all circles says
We just must just adjust.

Jaak - Adjusted, May, 2015

151

Homeward Bound, Philippines

A New Jeepney Chassis, Road to Manila, Philippines

ABOUT THE AUTHOR

The author was a sailor that spent two years aboard a 'Kilauea Class' Ammunition ship (USS Flint, AE-32), as a Machinist Mate Petty Officer assigned to 'A' Gang (Auxiliaries), and 'R' Division, on three separate 'WESPAC' cruises in the Pacific, South China Seas, Indian Ocean, and other ports west, between March 1973 and March 1975.

Upon discharge from active duty, the author returned to college on the GI Bill, earning a Mechanical Engineering degree (BSE) from Western Michigan University in 1978, and 'Master of Business' MBA degree in 1988,… then working in a variety of Engineering, Marketing, and Management positions until starting his own business. As a 'Project Engineer' working for a large manufacturing company in Milwaukee, he spent six years in design, manufacturing, testing, and 'start up' of desalination plants, ASME code pressure vessels, and process equipment for US Navy, marine, and commercial ship applications. Working with the company under a NAVSEA contract, he developed the first Reverse Osmosis Desalination plant for US Navy Combatant ships during the mid 1980's, installed the unit aboard a US Navy Destroyer in Norfolk, Virginia, and rode the ship to Puerto Rico with the crew in 1987 to prove the concept. Jaak Tallinn lives in Wisconsin, and has been self-employed in his own 'Business Development Consulting' company since 1991.